*The
Dalai Lama's
Book of
Daily Meditations*

Also available from Rider . . .

The Dalai Lama's Book of Wisdom
edited by Matthew E. Bunson

The
Dalai Lama's
Book of
Daily Meditations

*

The Path to Tranquillity

Compiled and Edited by Renuka Singh
With a Foreword by the Dalai Lama

RIDER
LONDON · SYDNEY · AUCKLAND · JOHANNESBURG

First published in 1998 by Viking, Penguin Books India (P) Ltd.
This edition published in 1999 by Rider.
an imprint of Ebury Press, Random House,
20 Vauxhall Bridge Road, London SW1V 2SA
www.randomhouse.co.uk

Random House Australia (Pty) Limited
20 Alfred Street, Milsons Point, Sydney,
New South Wales 2061, Australia

Random House New Zealand Limited
18 Poland Road, Glenfield,
Auckland 10, New Zealand

Random House (Pty) Limited
Endulini, 5A Jubilee Road,
Parktown 2193, South Africa

The Random House Group Limited Reg. No. 954009

Pages vii to viii constitute an extension of the copyright page.

Papers used by Rider are natural, recyclable products made from
wood grown in sustainable forests.

Printed and bound by Mackays of Chatham

A CIP catalogue record for this book
is available from the British Library

ISBN 0-7126-0898-2

CONTENTS

Acknowledgements   *vii*
Foreword   *ix*
Editor's Note   *xi*

January   1
February   35
March   67
April   101
May   133
June   167
July   199
August   233
September   267
October   299
November   333
December   365

Index   *399*

ACKNOWLEDGEMENTS

Grateful acknowledgement is made for permission to reprint the following copyright material:

From *Gentle Bridges* by Jeremy W. Hayward and Francisco J. Verela © 1992. Reprinted by arrangement with Shambhala Publications Inc., Boston.

From *A Flash of Lightning in the Dark of Night* by the Dalai Lama © 1994 by Association Bouddhiste des Centres de Dordogne. Reprinted by arrangement with Shambhala Publications Inc., Boston.

From *Violence and Compassion: Conversations with the Dalai Lama*, translated by Jean Claude Carriere. Translation copyright © 1996 Doubleday a division of Bantam Doubleday Dell Publishing Group. Used by permission of Doubleday a division of Bantam Doubleday Dell Publishing Group, Inc.

From *Mandala* magazine. Reprinted by arrangement with Foundation for the Preservation of the Mahayana Tradition (FPMT) International Office, California, publisher of *Mandala* magazine.

From *Kindness, Clarity and Insight*, edited by Jeffrey Hopkins and Elizabeth Napper © 1988; *Path of the Bodhisattva Warrior* by Glenn H. Mullin © 1988; *Path to Bliss*, edited by Christine Cox © 1991; *A Policy of Kindness*, edited by Sidney Piburn © 1993 (2nd edition); *Healing Anger* by the Dalai Lama © 1997. Reprinted by arrangement with Snow Lion Publications, New York.

From *Generous Wisdom*, edited by Dexter Roberts © 1992; *Dialogues on Universal Responsibility and Education* by H.H. the Dalai Lama © 1995; *Opening the Mind and Generating a*

ACKNOWLEDGEMENTS

Good Heart by H.H. the Dalai Lama © 1995 (4th edition). Reprinted by arrangement with the Library of Tibetan Works and Archives, Dharamsala.

From *Collected Statements, Interviews and Articles: H.H. the XIV Dalai Lama* © 1986. Reprinted by arrangement with the Department of Information and International Relations, Dharamsala.

From *Mind Science* by the Dalai Lama © 1991; *The Dalai Lama: The Meaning of Life*, edited by Jeffrey Hopkins © 1992; *The World of Tibetan Buddhism* by the Dalai Lama, edited by Geshe Thupten Jinpa* © 1995; *The Good Heart* by H.H. the Dalai Lama, edited by Robert Kiely © 1996; *Sleeping, Dreaming and Dying*, edited by Francisco J. Verela © 1997. Reprinted by arrangement with Wisdom Publications, New York.

From *Freedom in Exile by the Dalai Lama of Tibet* © 1990. Published by Hodder & Stoughton, London.

From *Worlds in Harmony* by the Dalai Lama with Daniel Goleman *et al* © 1992. Published by Parallax Press, California.

From *Dharma Celebration Lectures*. Reprinted by arrangement with Tushita Mahayana Meditation Centre, Delhi.

FOREWORD

THE DALAI LAMA

As human beings, we all want to be happy and to avoid suffering. In my limited experience, if we are to achieve this, it is immensely valuable to be able to cultivate and maintain a positive state of mind. In the Buddhist tradition to which I belong, one of the most effective means of doing so is to engage in meditation. However, although meditation can sometimes mean sitting in a particular formal posture and stilling the mind, it can also include continuously familiarizing ourselves with positive thoughts. This is why we regularly read and recite the texts of scriptures and prayers. I myself have drawn great inspiration over the years from a short work called 'Eight Verses for Training the Mind'. It contains much useful advice, counselling us always to consider others as more important than ourselves, to face and oppose the disturbing emotions that endanger our peace of mind and to give whatever benefit arises to others, while shouldering whatever difficulties occur on ourselves.

This book contains daily quotations selected from my own writings and published works. I humbly pray that readers may find some inspiration in them to develop that warm hearted peace of mind that is the key to enduring happiness.

26 February 1998

This book is a compilation of daily thoughts by His Holiness the Dalai Lama. It also forms a part of His Holiness's contribution to the preservation of the ancient Indian wisdom-culture. My publisher originally proposed the idea behind this book and His Holiness gave this project his approval and blessing. I began working on it without delay at the beginning of last year.

I am acutely aware of the principle of selectivity unfolding here. The quotations are my selections from His Holiness's writings, teachings and occasional interviews. These, I hope, will properly reflect His Holiness's spiritual and secular concerns and spread his message of universal responsibility, compassion and peace. Also, through these quotations, I intend to share with non-specialized audiences and Dharma students the different vistas and possibilities that opened before me, and the apparently simple yet complex core of His Holiness's essential thoughts. However, one must bear in mind that terms such as 'listening', 'giving', 'thinking', 'meditating' etc. are processual and should be perceived in the context of the Buddhist practice of cultivating bodhicitta, i.e., the aspiration to attain enlightenment for the benefit of all.

In the foreword, His Holiness very aptly refers to the 'Eight Verses for Training the Mind'. Based on my personal experiences, I can also vouch for their unfailing usefulness and would like to present the verses here:

Regarding all sentient beings
As excelling even the wish-granting gem
For accomplishing the highest aim,
May I always hold them most dear.

When in the company of others
I shall always consider myself the lowest of all,
And from the depth of my heart
Hold them dear and supreme.

Vigilant, the moment a delusion appears,
Which endangers myself and others,

I shall confront and avert it
Without delay.

When I see beings of wicked nature
overwhelmed by violent negative actions and
                                    sufferings,
I shall hold such rare ones dear,
As if I have found a precious treasure.

When others, out of envy, treat me with abuse,
Insult me or the like,
I shall accept defeat,
And offer the victory to others.

When someone I have benefited
And in whom I have great hopes
Gives me terrible harm,
I shall regard him as my holy spiritual friend.

In short, both directly and indirectly, do I offer
Every benefit and happiness to all sentient beings,
                                    my mothers;
May I secretly take upon myself
All their harmful actions and suffering.

May they not be defiled by the concepts
Of the eight profane concerns.
And aware that all things are illusory,
May they, ungrasping, be freed from bondage.

I am deeply indebted to my teacher and

friend His Holiness Tenzin Gyatso, the fourteenth Dalai Lama, for his support and blessings for this project. For all his cooperation and patience, Tenzin Geyche Tethong deserves a special thanks. I also owe thanks to Lhakdor for his promptness in providing me with His Holiness's unpublished material and for his valuable suggestions.

I extend my gratitude to Linda and Ashok Jhalani, Antonella and Naresh Mathur, and Alison Ramsey for confirming some of my selections in this book. Also to Prama and Ranji Bhandari for their moral support, and to Sunita Kakaria for taking care of me in McLeod Ganj. I would also like to acknowledge the help rendered by V.K. Karthika and Sudeshna Shome Ghosh from Penguin. They have been working painstakingly on this project with me. At the eleventh hour, receiving financial support from Derek Goh for seeking permission to publish the selected quotations came as a real surprise. I am grateful to him for not letting this project fall apart.

EDITOR'S NOTE

Finally, thanks to my family members Pritam Singh, Jyoti and Paul, Ashma and Tsagaadai, and Sumeet and Supriti for their support that allowed me to devote so much time to my work.

This work is dedicated to all sentient beings with a wish for their welfare and happiness.

Renuka Singh
April 1998

January

I love friends,
I want more friends. I love smiles.
That is a fact.
How to develop smiles? There are a
variety of smiles. Some smiles are
sarcastic. Some smiles are artificial —
diplomatic smiles.
These smiles do not produce
satisfaction, but rather fear or
suspicion. But a genuine smile gives us
hope, freshness.
If we want a genuine smile, then first
we must produce
the basis for a smile to come.

*I*f you have fear of some pain or
suffering, you should examine whether
there is anything you can do about it.
If you can, there is no need
to worry about it;
if you cannot do anything,
then also there is no need
to worry.

*T*o be aware of a single shortcoming
within oneself is more useful
than to be aware of a thousand
in somebody else. Rather than
speaking badly about people
and in ways that will produce friction
and unrest in their lives,
we should practise a purer perception
of them, and when we speak of others,
speak of their good qualities.
If you find yourself slandering anybody,
first imagine that your mouth is filled
with excrement. It will break you
of the habit quickly enough.

*I*f you are mindful of death,
it will not come as a surprise — you will
not be anxious.
You will feel that death is
merely like changing your clothes.
Consequently, at that point
you will be able to maintain
your calmness of mind.

*T*o foster inner
awareness, introspection and
reasoning is more efficient than
meditation and prayer.

*R*ight from the moment of our birth,
we are under the care
and kindness of our parents
and then later on in our life
when we are oppressed by sickness
and become old,
we are again dependent
on the kindness of others.
Since at the beginning
and end of our lives
we are so dependent on
others' kindness, how can it be
that in the middle
we neglect kindness towards others?

Scientific research and development
should work together with
meditative research and development
since both are concerned
with similar objects.
The one proceeds through
experiment by instruments, and the other
through inner experience and meditation.
A clear distinction should be made
between what is not found by science and
what is found to be non-existent by science.
What science finds to be non-existent,
we must accept as non-existent,
but what science merely does not find
is a completely different matter . . .
It is quite clear that there are
many, many mysterious things.

All of the different religious faiths,
despite their philosophical differences,
have a similar objective. Every religion
emphasizes human improvement, love,
respect for others, sharing other
people's suffering. On these lines every
religion has more or less the same
viewpoint and the same goal.

*P*hysically you are a human being,
but mentally you are incomplete.
Given that we have this
physical human form,
we must safeguard our mental
capacity for judgement.
For that, we cannot take out insurance;
the insurance company is within:
self-discipline, self-awareness,
and a clear realization
of the disadvantages of anger
and the positive effects of kindness.

*I*n the case of one individual
or person like myself, the practice
of compassion and religion
coincides, but another individual,
without religion, can practise
spirituality without being religious.
So, a secular person can be spiritual.
Compassion is compulsory
for everyone to practice,
and if I were a dictator
I would dictate to everyone
to do so.

I think religion, ideology, economy and
political systems are all man's creation.
Since they are man's creation, they
must relate with human feeling
and the human spirit. If they are
practised with human feeling, they fulfil
some basic human aspirations.
The various religions and ideologies
are meant for humanity
and not the opposite.

Material progress alone is not
sufficient to achieve an ideal society.
Even in countries where great external
progress has been made, mental
problems have increased. No amount of
legislation or coercion can accomplish
the well-being of society, for this
depends upon the internal attitude of
the people who comprise it. Therefore,
mental development, in harmony with
material development,
is very important.

The human level of mental development is not complete. Even in the ordinary sense, within our inner state there are still many things to explore. This has nothing to do with religious ideology, this is spiritual. Some part of the brain's capability may be fully utilized only through deep meditation. But in the meantime, things can be explored in the ordinary way. So from that viewpoint, the human being is unfinished.

Sometimes one creates
a dynamic impression
by saying something,
and sometimes one creates
as significant an impression
by remaining silent.

*A*ll living beings, starting from
insects, want happiness
and not suffering.
However, we are only one,
whereas others are infinite in number.
Thus, it can be clearly decided
that others gaining happiness
is more important than
just yourself alone.

*I*f during the dreaming state
you direct your awareness
and your concentration to the throat,
this will make your dreams clearer.
Whereas, if you direct your awareness
to the heart, then it will
make your sleep deeper.
So here is a subjective sleeping pill.

*I*t would be much more constructive
if people tried to understand
their supposed enemies.
Learning to forgive is much more useful
than merely picking up a stone
and throwing it at the object
of one's anger, the more so when
the provocation is extreme.
For it is under the greatest
adversity that there exists
the greatest potential
for doing good, both for
oneself and others.

*T*o develop patience,
you need someone who wilfully hurts
you. Such people give us real
opportunities to practise tolerance.
They test our inner strength in a way
that even our guru cannot. Basically,
patience protects us from being
discouraged.

Whether in remote places
or densely populated cities, we work
and struggle for the same fundamental
purpose. While doing so, we fail to
realize that it is important to follow the
correct method in achieving our
goal—for the method
is all important.

When a faulty deed has been done,
then after learning that it was wrong,
one can engage in disclosure
of the faulty deed (in the presence of
actual or imagined holy beings)
and develop an intention not to do
that action again in the future.
This diminishes the force of the ill deed.

On the basis of external action,
it is difficult to distinguish
whether an action is violent or
non-violent. Basically it depends on
the motivation behind the action.
If the motivation is negative,
even though the external appearance
may be very smooth and gentle, in a
deeper sense the action is very violent.
On the contrary, harsh actions
and words done with a sincere,
positive motivation are
essentially non-violent.
In other words, violence is
a destructive power.
Non-violence is constructive.

I tell my generation that
we were born during the darkest
period in our long history.
There is a big challenge and it is very
unfortunate. But if there is a challenge
then there is an opportunity to face it,
an opportunity to demonstrate
our will and our determination.
So from that viewpoint I think
that our generation is fortunate.

*T*o develop genuine devotion, you must know the meaning of teachings. The main emphasis in Buddhism is to transform the mind, and transformation dependes upon meditation. In order to meditate correctly you must have knowledge, and communities, too, must be uplifted through knowledge.

*K*indness is the key to peace and
harmony in family life. Families in exile
must educate their children. They
should be their first lama.

A blossoming tree becomes bare and stripped in autumn. Beauty changes into ugliness, youth into old age, and fault into virtue. Things do not remain the same and nothing really exists. Thus, appearances and emptiness exist simultaneously.

*D*etermination, courage and
self-confidence are the key factors for
success. In spite of obstacles and
difficulties, if we have firm
determination, we can work them out.
Whatever the circumstances, we should
remain humble, modest
and without pride.

We can hardly call a beggar an
obstacle to generosity.

Simply being praised is of no substantial help at all: it does not increase people's good fortune, nor does it make them live any longer. If temporary pleasure is all you want you might as well take drugs. Yet many people invest much money and even deceive their friends so as to win status. This is quite stupid. Their status and fame do not really help much in this life and do nothing for future lives. There is no point in being happy if we are famous, or unhappy because people speak ill of us.

*I*t is said that
if you want to know
what you were doing in the past,
look at your body now;
if you want to know
what will happen
to you in the future,
look at what
your mind is doing now.

*R*eligion involves practice of methods and modes conducive to the realization of serenity, discipline, joyous detachment and self-control. It should be observed that normally it is through the inattentive body, speech and mind that all harmful and unethical conditions are created. Therefore, it naturally presupposes that the pacification, training and taming of the physical, mental and verbal activities are of fundamental importance.
To sum up, it is essential first of all to rectify, nullify and put a stop to all physical misconduct, followed by that of speech.

*P*oliticians need religion even more than a hermit in retreat. If a hermit acts out of bad motivation, he harms no one but himself. But if someone who can directly influence the whole of society acts with bad motivation, then a great number of people will be adversely affected.

February

*T*o renounce the world means
to give up your attachment
to the world. It does not mean
that you have to separate yourself
from it. The very purpose of our doctrine
is to serve others. In order to serve
others you must remain in the
society. You should not isolate
yourself from the rest.

*H*uman happiness and human
satisfaction must ultimately
come from within oneself.
It is wrong to expect some final
satisfaction to come from
money or from a computer.

According to Buddhist practice,
basically there are three stages
or steps. The initial stage is
to reduce attachment towards life.
The second stage is the
elimination of desire and
attachment to this samsara.
Then in the third stage,
self-cherishing is eliminated.
As a result of rigorous practice
I feel there is a possibility
of cessation, i.e. nirvana.

*T*rue compassion is not just an
emotional response but a firm
commitment founded on reason.
Therefore, a truly compassionate
attitude towards others does not change
even if they behave negatively.
Through universal altruism, you
develop a feeling of responsibility for
others: the wish to help them actively
overcome their problems.

*F*or discovering one's true inner nature, I think one should try to take out some time, with quiet and relaxation, to think more inwardly and to investigate the inner world. That may help. Then sometimes when one is very much involved in hatred or attachment, if there is time or possibility during that very moment, just try to look inward and ask: 'What is attachment? What is the nature of anger?'

*S*uffering increases your inner strength. Also, the wishing for suffering makes the suffering disappear.

*I*f the basic human nature was aggressive, we would have been born with animal claws and huge teeth — but ours are very short, very pretty, very weak! That means we are not well equipped to be aggressive beings. Even the size of our mouth is very small. So, I think the basic nature of human beings should be gentle.

*D*uring conception, even the physical substance on which the self is conventionally based — the egg and sperm — belongs to someone else, the parents, still you can say that it belongs to the self also. The body comes from someone else, but as soon as the consciousness enters, it's that new person's body, embryo, foetus, or whatever you want to call it, even though prior to that it wasn't. So, the physical constituents of the embryo come from two different people, but as soon as the consciousness enters the mixed cell, that cell now belongs to the consciousness.

*A*s long as you are not completely enlightened there will always be an inner obstruction to knowledge that will make your task of helping others incomplete.

Among the 5.7 billion human beings, the older generation, including me, is getting ready to say goodbye to this world. The youth has to carry the responsibility for the future. So, please realize your responsibilty, remember your potential, and have self-confidence. Have an open mind and a sense of caring and belonging. The freshness and strength that youth has, should not fade away. You must keep this enthusiasm.

*L*aziness will stop your progress in your spiritual practice. One can be deceived by three types of laziness: the laziness of indolence, which is the wish to procrastinate; the laziness of inferiority, which is doubting your capabilities; and the laziness that is attachment to negative actions, or putting great effort into non-virtue.

*I*deally, one should have
a great deal of courage and strength
but not boast about, or make a big show
of it. Then, in times of need, one should
rise to the occasion and fight bravely
for what is right.

*S*ome people, sweet and attractive,
and strong and healthy, happen to die
young. They are masters in disguise
teaching us about impermanence.

We practise various meditations during dream states. The potential of such practices is that at a certain level it is possible to separate the gross levels of consciousness from the gross physical state, and arrive at a subtler level of mind and body. You could, for example, separate your mind from your body during sleep and do some extra work that you cannot do in your ordinary body. However, you might not get paid for it!

*O*ur state of mind plays
a major role in our day-to-day
experiences as well as our physical and
mental well-being. If a person has a
calm and stable mind, this influences
his or her attitude and behaviour in
relation to others. In other words, if
someone remains in a peaceful and
tranquil state of mind, external
surroundings can cause them only a
limited disturbance.

*N*early all of us receive
our first lessons in peaceful living
from our mothers, because the need
for love lies at the very foundation of
human existence. From the earliest
stages of our growth, we are completely
dependent upon our mother's care and
it is very important for us that she
express her love. If children do not
receive proper affection, in later life
they will often find it hard
to love others.

*I*f objects and people
evoke attachment in us, we do not
understand the true nature of
phenomena. We can only become
detached by realizing the true
nature of things.

*H*ere is a general statement
about Tibetan medicine:
Human physiology is spoken of in terms
of the three humours — wind, bile and
phlegm. Where do disturbances
originate? Wind, bile and phlegm
imbalances occur respectively, from the
'three poisons', or primary mental
afflictions, namely attachment, anger
and ignorance.

Both bondage and true freedom
depend on the varying states
of the clear light mind.
The state that meditators
try to attain through the application of
various meditative techniques is one in
which this ultimate nature of
mind fully manifests all
its positive potential.

*E*very noble work is bound
to face problems and obstacles.
It is important to check your goal
and motivation thoroughly. One should
be very truthful, honest and reasonable.
One's action should be good for others,
and for oneself as well. Once a
positive goal is chosen, you should
decide to pursue it all the
way to the end. Even if
it is not realized, at least
there will be no regret.

*E*verything has its limits.
Too much consumption or effort to
make money is not good. Neither is
too much contentment. In principle,
contentment should be pursued,
but pure contentment
is almost suicidal.

What irritates us in the first place
is that our wishes are not fulfilled.
But remaining upset does nothing
to help fulfil those wishes.
So we neither fulfil our wishes nor
regain our cheerfulness! This
disconcerted state, from which anger
can grow, is most dangerous.
We should try never to let
our happy frame of mind be disturbed.
Whether we are suffering
at present or have suffered in the
past, there is no reason
to be unhappy.

When you have fear,
you can think: 'Others have fear
similar to this, may I take to myself
all of their fears.'
Even though you are opening yourself
to greater suffering, taking greater
hardship on yourself,
your fear lessens.

*I*n this ever-changing world there are
two important things that we should
keep in mind. The first is
self-examination. We should re-examine
our own attitude towards others and
constantly check ourselves
to see whether we are practising
properly. Before pointing our finger
at others we should point it
towards ourselves. Secondly, we must
be prepared to admit our faults and
stand corrected.

Your experience will enable you to understand what 'consciousness' implies and what it is. Consciousness is a non-obstructing phenomenon, is non-material, and has the quality of luminosity, that is, it reflects any object by arising in the aspect of that object. Consciousness is like a crystal stone; while a crystal is resting on a coloured surface, you cannot see the real untinted clarity of the crystal stone, but once you take the crystal away from the surface, you can perceive its actual clarity.

*I*ndividuals who are best suited
for practice are those who are
not only intellectually gifted,
but also have single-pointed faith
and dedication and are wise.
These people are most receptive to
spiritual practice. In the second group,
individuals may not be highly
intelligent, but they have a rock-solid
foundation in faith. The unfortunate
are those in the third category.
Although these individuals may be
highly intelligent, they are always
dogged by scepticism and doubts. They
are clever, but they tend to be hesitant
and sceptical and are never really able
to settle down. These people are
the least receptive.

*I*f you want to change the world,
first try to improve and bring about
change within yourself. That will
help change your family. From there
it just gets bigger and bigger.
Everything we do has some
effect, some impact.

*T*he idea that our interactions with others actually help our own insight is quite interesting. In an intimate relationship, where love and attachment are mixed, it is difficult to say how this will help the individual who is practising. In a case where there is attachment or clinging to another person, where the person is arising as a very strong object and the attachment is arising with a strong sense of 'I' — 'I love this person, I am grasping for this person' — if you see this as a false idea of self, you can have some insight into the notion of emptiness.

A nagging sense of discontent,
a feeling of being dissatisfied, or
of something being not right,
is the fuel that gives rise to anger
and hatred. This discontent arises in us
when we feel that either we ourselves,
or someone we love, or our close friends,
are being treated unfairly or threatened,
and that people are being unjust. Also,
when others somehow obstruct us in
achieving something, we feel that we
are being trodden upon, and then we
feel angry. So the approach here is
to get at the root, appreciating
the causal nexus, the chain,
which will ultimately explode
in an emotional state
like anger or hatred.

March

Whether one believes
in a religion or not, and
whether one believes in rebirth
or not, there isn't anyone
who doesn't appreciate kindness
and compassion.

When we consider that
everything we experience results
from a complex interplay of causes
and conditions, we find that there is no
single thing to desire or resent and it is
more difficult for the afflictions of
attachment and anger to arise. In this
way the view of interdependence
makes our minds more
relaxed and open.

On the subject of love
and marriage, my simple opinion
is that making love is alright, but for
marriage, don't hurry, be cautious.
Make sure you will remain together
forever, at least for this whole life. That
is important, for if you marry hurriedly
without understanding well what you
are doing, then after a month or after a
year, trouble starts and you will be
seeking divorce. From a legal viewpoint
divorce is possible, and without
children maybe it is acceptable,
but with children, it is not.

When we contemplate death
and the impermanence of life, our
minds automatically begin to take an
interest in spiritual achievements,
just as an ordinary person becomes
apprehensive upon seeing the corpse
of a friend. Meditation on death
cuts off attraction toward transient
and meaningless activities.

*T*ry to develop a deep conviction that
the present human body has great
potential and that you shall never
waste even a single minute of its use.
Not taking any essence of this precious
human existence, but just wasting it, is
almost like taking poison while being
fully aware of the consequences of
doing so. It is very wrong for people
to feel deeply sad when they lose
some money, while when they waste
the precious moments of their lives
they do not have the slightest feeling
of repentance.

The world today is engulfed in conflicts and sufferings to such an extent that everyone longs for peace and happiness; that longing has unfortunately led them to be carried away by the pursuit of ephemeral pleasures. But there are a few learned people who, dissatisfied by what is ordinarily seen or experienced, think more deeply and search for true happiness. I believe that the search for Truth will continue and will grow even keener as we make greater material progress.

*H*uman potential is the same for all.
Your feeling, 'I am of no value', is
wrong. Absolutely wrong. You are
deceiving yourself. We all have
the power of thought — so what are you
lacking? If you have will-power,
then you can do anything.
It is usually said that you
are your own master.

We need to develop patience but impatience can also be conducive for such activities as cleaning and walking. With this mind of impatience one can become a woman or man of action. However, for bigger problems, patience is crucial.

*I*f one's life is simple,
contentment has to come.
Simplicity is extremely important
for happiness. Having few desires,
feeling satisfied with what you have,
is very vital: satisfaction with just
enough food, clothing, shelter
to protect yourself from the
elements. And finally, there is an
intense delight in abandoning
faulty states of mind and in
cultivating helpful ones
in meditation.

According to the Latin root of the word, 'religion' would mean 'to bind again'. Now how does the concept of binding or tying up come to be applied as the common term for all our various teachings? The common enemy of all religious disciplines, the target of all moral precepts laid down by the great teachers of mankind, is selfishness of mind. For it is just this which causes ignorance, anger and passion which are at the root of all the troubles of the world.

According to tantra, the ultimate nature of mind is essentially pure. This pristine nature is technically called 'clear light'. When this clear light nature of mind is veiled or inhibited from expressing its true essence by the conditioning of afflictive emotions and thoughts, the person is said to be caught in the cycle of existence, samsara. But when, by applying appropriate meditative techniques and practices, the individual is able to fully experience this clear light nature of mind, free from the influence of the afflictive states, he or she is on the way to true liberation and full enlightenment.

Subconscious anger, if it has
a parallel in Buddhist writings, would
have more to do with what is called
mental unhappiness or dissatisfaction,
in the sense that they are regarded as
the sources of anger and hostility. We
can see it in terms of a lack of
awareness, as well as an active
misconstruing of reality.

Compassion, tolerance and altruism
bring us happiness and calmness.
Therefore, these are basically spiritual.
Religion comes later. Actually religion
is meant for satisfaction and is the
ultimate source of happiness. It simply
tries to strengthen the element of
mental happiness. Perhaps positive
mental thought is my
conception of spirituality.

*T*oday our knowledge has expanded
greatly with the help of science and
technology. But knowledge regarding
our own mind, our deep nature,
is still limited in the Western world.
This is because consciousness is
formless and cannot be touched
and so cannot be measured
with instruments. It can only
be known through
meditation and other methods.

We find that between
the past and the future there is an
extremely thin line — something that
cannot really withstand analysis. Past and
future exist in relation to the present. But
if the present cannot be posited, how can
past and future be posited? This is a
demonstration of dependent
origination.

At the moment when
strong feelings of anger arise,
no matter how hard one tries
to adopt a dignified pose,
one's face looks rather ugly.
The vibration that person sends
is very hostile. People can sense it,
and it is almost as if one can feel
steam coming out of that person's body.
Indeed, not only are human beings
capable of sensing it, but
pets and other animals also
try to avoid that person
at that instant.

*I*f the evolution of the human species is
entirely a matter of the environment
and the modification of genes,
chromosomes, and so forth, then there
really isn't place for Karma at all. It
simply wouldn't fit because all the
effects would presumably be entirely
accounted for by their physical
constituents. However, cells evolve to
become more and more complex
and then later evolve into human
beings. There are many options, some
seventy trillion, that one human
could become, based on the assortment
of the parental genes. Yet just one
option is taken, and if the question is
asked—why? then Karma
is directly related
to this question.

*H*appiness is a state of mind.
With physical comforts
if your mind is still in a state
of confusion and agitation,
it is not happiness.
Happiness means calmness of mind.

Sexual desire, by definition, wants something: the satisfaction of desire by the possession of the other. To a large extent this is a mental projection, provoked by a certain emotion. We imagine the other in our possession. At the moment of desire everything seems agreeable and desirable. One sees no obstacle to it, no reason for restraint. The object desired seems to have no defects, to be worthy of all praise. But then everything changes with possession. Once the desire disappears — whether it considers itself satisfied, or time passes and weakens it — we no longer look at the other in the same way. Some people admit they are stunned by this. Each one discovers the true nature of the other. That is why there are so many broken marriages, quarrels, lawsuits, so much hatred.

*T*he image we have
of ourselves readily tends to be
complacent. We look at ourselves
with indulgence. When something
unpleasant happens to us, we always
have the tendency to cast the blame
on others, or on fate, a demon,
or a god. We shrink from
descending into ourselves,
as the Buddha recommended.

*I*t looks like there is
an awful lot of work to do. If you had to
analyse all your dreams there would be
no time left to dream.

*I*f an individual has a sufficient spiritual base, he won't let himself be overwhelmed by the lure of technology and by the madness of possession. He or she will know how to find the right balance, without asking for too much, and know how to say: I have a camera, that's enough, I don't want another. The constant danger is to open the door to greed, one of our most relentless enemies. It is here that the real work of the mind is put into practice.

*F*or a bodhisattva to be
successful in accomplishing the practice
of the six perfections — generosity,
ethical discipline, tolerance, joyous
effort, concentration and wisdom —
cooperation with, and kindness
towards, fellow beings are
extremely important.

Years back when I drove along the road to the airport or somewhere else, I never saw chickens in the streets, in the shop fronts of stores or restaurants.
Now I see them everywhere.
But why these rows of slaughtered chickens?
Although it is impossible to be a total vegetarian in Tibet, I find killing animals repugnant. As far as possible I eat only vegetables and fruits.

*T*he mind, whose nature
we realize in order to actualize
omniscience, must be a very
special type of mind, which,
in terms of its continuity,
is eternal. It cannot be any other
type of mind. Because the
various contaminated states of mind,
such as delusions and afflictive
emotional and cognitive states are
adventitious, they are occasional:
they arise in a certain moment
but soon disappear and
are not enduring.

Suffering originates from
various causes and conditions. But the
root cause of our pain and suffering lies
in our own ignorant and undisciplined
state of mind. The happiness we seek
can be attained only through the
purification of our minds.

*I*n our world, we need
a clear awareness of the interdependent
nature of nations, of humans and
animals, and of humans, animals and
the world. Everthing is of
interdependent nature. I feel that many
problems, especially man-made
problems, are due to a lack of
knowledge about this
interdependent nature.

*I*t is because of the intimate
relationship between mind and body,
and the existence of special
physiological centres within our body,
that physical yoga exercises and the
application of special meditative
techniques aimed at training
the mind can have positive
effects on health.

*T*o stop being born in cyclic existence,
meditate on the path; even if your head
is on fire engage in practice and don't
take time to put out the fire.

When we take the Buddha as an authority, as a reliable teacher, we do so on the basis of having investigated and examined his principal teaching, the Four Noble Truths. It is after having investigated the validity and reliability of this doctrine that we accept the Buddha, who propounded it, as a reliable teacher.

*O*ne important type of charity is
the giving of material things such as
food, clothing and shelter to others,
but it is limited, for it does not bring
complete satisfaction. Just as our own
experience confirms that through
gradual purification of our minds
more and more happiness develops,
so it is the same for others;
thus it is crucial that they understand
what they should adopt in practice
in order to achieve happiness.
To facilitate their learning these topics,
we need to be fully capable
of teaching them.

April

*I*t is necessary to help others,
not only in our prayers, but in
our daily lives. If we find
we cannot help others,
the least we can do is to desist
from harming them.

*T*he observation that good people suffer, and evil people keep enjoying benefits and recognition, is short-sighted. Also, this kind of conclusion might have been made in haste. If one analyses carefully, one finds that troublemakers are definitely not happy. It is better to behave well and take responsibility for one's actions, and lead a positive life.

I have found that the greatest
degree of inner tranquillity
comes from the development
of love and compassion.
The more we care for
the happiness of others, the greater
is our own sense of well-being.
Cultivating a close, warm-
hearted feeling for others
automatically puts the mind
at ease. It is the ultimate
source of success in life.

*I*t seems to me that Western science and Eastern philosophy can join together to create a really complete and full-fledged human being. It is only in this way that man will emerge strengthened from his condition and become whole. What in fact interests me is what is beyond matter and awareness, what really is important and what makes us what we are.

I understand the meaning of 'open' as
just like an open door; it can open
very easily, without difficulty.
'Free' is also the same.
As a result of being free
and open, the more you receive new
ideas, it makes you want to give out
more of your energy.
That way, each helps the other.
It is very useful, very necessary,
especially these days.

The grosser consciousness depends heavily on particles of matter. The subtler consciousness is more independent — it does not depend so much on the brain. In the Buddha state, the grosser mind completely disappears. Luminance, radiance, imminence — the three states of subtle mind — all of these disappear in the clear light, the innermost consciousness.

*T*he Fully Enlightened One said
that all he can do is teach us
the Dharma, the path to liberation from
suffering; it is up to us to put it into
practice — he washed his hands
of that responsibility!

*B*odhicitta is the medicine which revives and gives life to every sentient being who even hears of it. When you engage in fulfilling the needs of others, your own needs are fulfilled as a by-product.

*T*aking your own body and mind as
the laboratory, engage in some
thoroughgoing research
on your own mental
functioning, and examine
the possibility of making
some positive changes
within yourself.

Such practices as bodhicitta automatically bring calmness at the time of death. The mind at the time of death is at a very critical period, and if you are able to leave a strong positive impact at that time, then it will become a very powerful force in continuing a positive experience in the next life.

*I*f in a competitive society
you are sincere and honest,
in some circumstances people
may take advantage of you.
If you let someone do so,
he or she will be engaging in an
unsuitable action and accumulating
bad Karma that will harm
the person in the future. Thus it is
permissible, with an altruistic
motivation, to take counteraction
in order to prevent the other person
from having to undergo
the effects of this
wrong action.

*T*hree qualities enable people to understand the teachings: objectivity, which means an open mind; intelligence, which is the critical faculty to discern the real meaning by checking the teachings of Buddha; and interest and commitment, which means enthusiasm.

A strong sense of separateness
in the past has brought about
competition and warring.
But now, we are
more interdependent. So we
need to communicate, hold
dialogues, and compromise.
It would be good to have
a bullet that searches for
and hits the real
troublemaker, which is
within us.

Whenever Buddhism has taken root
in a new land there has always been a
certain variation in the style in which it
is observed. The Buddha himself taught
differently according to the place,
the occasion, and the situation of those
who were listening to him. So, all of us
have a great responsibility to take
the essence of Buddhism and
put it into practice in
our own lives.

*E*mptiness should be
understood in the context of
dependent arising and it should evoke a
sense of fullness, of things created by
causes and conditions. We shouldn't
think that the self is something that is
originally there and then eliminated
in meditation; in fact, it is
something that never
existed in the
first place.

*N*atural environment sustains the life
of all beings universally. Trees are
referred to in accounts of
the principal events of Buddha's life.
His mother leaned against a tree for
support as she gave birth to him.
He attained enlightenment seated
beneath a tree, and finally passed away
as trees stood witness overhead.

Whatever we say, let us speak clearly
and to the point, in a voice that is calm
and pleasant, unaffected by attachment
or hatred. Look kindly at others,
thinking : It is thanks to them that I
shall attain Buddhahood.

*I*f we are very forbearing,
then something we would normally
consider very painful will not appear so
bad after all. But without patient
endurance, even the smallest thing
becomes unbearable. A lot depends
on our attitude.

One of the things that meditation
teaches us, when we slowly descend
into ourselves, is that the sense of peace
already exists in us. We all have a deep
desire for it even if it's often hidden,
masked, thwarted. If we examine
human nature carefully, it is good, well
disposed, helpful. And it seems to me
that nowadays the spirit of harmony is
increasing, that our desire to live
together calmly is growing stronger and
stronger; it's more and more
widespread.

*I*t may surprise you, perhaps,
but I am not strictly opposed to
the spectacle of violence and crime.
It all depends on the lessons
you draw from it.

A good heart is both important
and effective in daily life. If in
a small family, even without children,
the members have a warm heart for
each other, a peaceful atmosphere
will be created. However, if one of
the persons feels angry, immediately
the atmosphere in the house
becomes tense. Despite good food
or a nice television set, you will lose
peace and calm. Thus things depend
more on the mind than on matter.
Matter is important, we must have it,
we must use it properly,
but in this century we must
combine a good brain
with a good heart.

All the problems that every individual
meets with in everyday life — famine,
unemployment, delinquency,
insecurity, psychological deviancy,
various epidemics, drugs, madness,
despair, terrorism — all that is
bound up with the widening gap
between the people, which,
needless to say, can also be found
inside the rich countries. Our ancient
experience confirms it at
every instant: everything is linked
together, everything is inseparable.
Consequently the gap
has to be reduced.

*T*he differences in physiology (skin
colour, slanted eyes, etc.) and culture
that appear to separate people, it seems
to me, only unify them all the more.
The theories of cultural difference
that the history of the world
has seen are absurd and pernicious.
They lead to nothing but bloody
impasses. Today especially, when
images from all over the earth are
coming our way, our deep unity
seems evident to me. Every new
institution ought to take this
as its point of departure,
as its foundation.

*I*f advertising is for a good cause,
it is worthwhile. Buddha
advertised enlightenment or nirvana.
If it is reasonable and beneficial,
it is good, but if it is only for profit,
cheating and exploitation
or is misleading, then
it is wrong.

Cultivating inner discipline is a
time-consuming process. Having
expectations of immediate results
is a sign of impatience. Ironically,
what the modern man wants
is the best, the fastest, the easiest, and,
if possible, the cheapest way.

*P*eople who fight with other human
beings out of anger, hatred and
strong emotion, even if they gain victory
over their enemies in battle, are not
in reality true heroes. What they
are doing is slaying corpses, because
human beings, being transient,
will die. Whether or not these
enemies die in the battle is
another question, but they will
die at some point. So, in reality,
they are slaying those already destined
to die. The true hero is the one
who gains victory over
hatred and anger.

*S*amsara — our conditioned
existence in the perpetual cycle of
habitual tendencies, and
nirvana — genuine freedom from such
an existence, are nothing but different
manifestations of a basic continuum.
So, this continuity of consciousness
is always present. This is
the meaning of tantra,
or continuity.

*I*f a patient is a believer,
terminal illness can be a
stepping-stone for personal growth
by following one's beliefs.
If one is a non-believer,
then friends need to show
a compassionate attitude as far
as possible, and share one's problems.

*T*he dying process begins with the dissolution of the elements within the body. It has eight stages, beginning with the dissolution of the earth element, then the water, fire, and wind element. This is followed by the experience of the next four stages which are visions in terms of colour: appearance of a white vision, increase of the red element, black near-attainment, and the clear light of death. In meditation, a practitioner is eventually able to experience the dissolution processes.

Nowadays the world is becoming
increasingly materialistic, and
mankind is reaching towards the very
zenith of external progress, driven by
an insatiable desire for power
and vast possessions. Yet by this
vain striving for perfection in a
world where everything is relative,
they wander ever further away
from inward peace and happiness
of the mind. This we can all bear
witness to, living as we do plagued
by unremitting anxiety in this
dreadful epoch of mammoth weapons.
It becomes more and more imperative
that the life of the spirit be
avowed as the only firm basis
upon which to establish
happiness and peace.

May

*T*he very purpose of religion is to control yourself, not to criticize others. Rather, we must criticize ourselves. How much am I doing about my anger? About my attachment, about my hatred, about my pride, my jealousy? These are the things which we must check in daily life.

We know that to wage
a nuclear war today, for example,
would be a form of suicide; or that to
pollute the air or the oceans
in order to achieve some short-term
benefit would be to destroy the
very basis for our survival.
As individuals and nations
are becoming increasingly
interdependent, we have no other
choice than to develop what
I call a sense of universal
responsibility.

*H*appiness is man's prerogative. He seeks it and each man is equally entitled to his pursuits of happiness; no man seeks misery. Justice and equality belong to man's prerogatives too, but these should derive their practice from altruism and should not have been corroded by the stations of power and wealth. To build such an altruistic motivation so that justice and equality may co-exist, the creation of a staunch moral fabric for the social environment is a prerequisite.

*I*deals are very important in one's life.
Without ideals you cannot move —
whether you achieve them
or not is immaterial.
But one must try and
approximate them.

A spoilt child, almost given up by the parents, who suddenly begins to act and behave well, pleases the parents to no end. Similarly, with proper reliance on the spiritual teacher, one can please the teacher and can quickly purify negativities.

*T*he ultimate authority must always rest with the individual's own reason and critical analysis.

We are born and reborn
countless number of times,
and it is possible that
each being has been our
parent at one time or another.
Therefore, it is likely that
all beings in this universe have
familial connections.

*I*n the Tibetan medical system
disorders of the flesh are related
to ignorance, disorders of the bones
to anger, and disorders of the
blood to attachment.

*S*words can be turned into ploughshares as has been mentioned in the Bible. It is a beautiful image, a weapon transformed into a tool to serve basic human needs, representing an attitude of inner and outer disarmament.

*I*t is often said that
you should make a thorough
examination of a potential guru, even
should it take twelve years.

The modern economy has no national
boundaries. When we talk about
ecology, the environment, when we are
concerned about the ozone layer, one
individual, one society, one country
cannot solve these problems. We must
work together. Humanity needs more
genuine cooperation. The foundation for
the development of good relations with
one another is altruism,
compassion and forgiveness.

I myself still occasionally become
irritated and angry and use harsh
words towards others. Then, a few
moments later when the anger has
subsided, I feel embarrassed;
the negative words are already spoken,
and there is no way to take them back.
Although the words have been uttered
and the sound of the voice has
ceased to exist, their impact still lives
on. Hence, the only thing I can do is to
go to the person and apologize,
isn't that right?

When I doubt that I exist,
I pinch myself. Even if
our knowledge of the world
and of ourselves is illusory,
a 'not-born', a 'not-become'
exists. Without it we
wouldn't exist. But we
exist in a way that
is at once relative (to the
activity of our mind) and
conditioned (by all the other
existences).

*I*f we consider material progress,
we see that research started
by one person can always
be continued by another.
But this is not possible
with spiritual progress. The
realization we talk about in the
Buddhadharma is something that
has to be accomplished by the
individual. No one else can do it for us.

There is a drunkenness from the power that we give ourselves over things. This drunkenness leads us to stop controlling our appetites. We want more and still more. Instead of quelling the fire, we reignite it. Instead of seeking inner disarmament, the only kind that counts, we multiply our tools of conquest. And we even forget to check whether the fulfilment of our desire is really the one we had wished for.

Good motivation causes good action. The beauty of action is in the method, and Buddhahood is the beauty of result. Generally beauty means something positive but if you are subjectively too attached to it and handle it wrongly, it can lead to destruction. But then I wonder about the definition of beauty. Can you consider the art of killing as beauty, especially painless killing? Or the art of warfare — little expense but a huge amount of destruction? Maybe it is considered as beauty.

*I*t is through listening that your mind
will turn with faith and devotion, and
you will be able to cultivate joy within
your mind and make your mind stable.
It is through listening that you will be
able to cultivate wisdom and be able to
remove ignorance. Therefore, it is
worthwhile to engage in listening even
if it costs your life. Listening is like a
torch that dispels the darkness of
ignorance. And if you are able to make
your mental continuum wealthy
through listening, no one can steal that
wealth. It is supreme wealth.

While you are engaging in the practice of giving you should do so with great happiness and radiance on your face. One should practice giving with a smile and with mental uprightness.

Compassion can be roughly defined
in terms of a state of mind
that is non-violent and
non-harming, or non-aggressive.
Because of this there is
a danger of confusing compassion
with attachment and intimacy.

We have genuine friendship when it is based on true human feeling, a feeling of closeness in which there is a sense of sharing and connectedness. I would call this type of friendship genuine because it is not affected by the increase or decrease of the individual's wealth, status, or power. The factor that sustains that friendship is whether or not the two people have mutual feelings of love and affection.

We should not be too concerned with our fame or what people say about us, either bad or good, because in reality fame could not make any serious difference to one's life. Therefore, we should have our priorities right, and seek what is truly of value, what is truly of meaning to our life, not just mere fame, which is, after all, empty sounds. Some individuals sacrifice many of their material possessions, wealth and even their lives to achieve fame. This type of obsession with seeking fame is very childish and is quite foolish.

You should see that all the external dirt and dust around you is basically a manifestation of the faults and stains within your mind. The most important aim is to purge these stains and faults from within your mind. Therefore, as you cleanse the environment, think that you are also purifying your mind.

Many people think that
to be patient in bearing loss
is a sign of weakness. I think
this is a mistake. It is
anger that is a sign of weakness,
whereas patience is a sign of strength.
For example, a person arguing a point
based on sound reasoning remains
confident and may even smile
while proving his case. On
the other hand, if his reasons
are unsound and he is about
to lose face, he gets angry, loses control
and starts talking nonsense. People
rarely get angry if they are
confident in what they are doing.
Anger comes more easily in
moments of confusion.

I used to feel that if I ever gain
a state of cessation, I shall really take
a good rest. Once we have attained
such a state, we could take a good
rest and a real holiday, in the true sense
of the word. Until we get to such
a state, it is foolish for us
to be complacent. When we
have attained the state of cessation,
we have truly reached a
very secure ground.

I find that there are two types of fear.
In one kind, things are quite delicate, or
critical. At such times, I know that I
must take a decision, whether I know
what to do or not. First, I try to consult
with my friends and reflect on it.
Then, I take a decision and act,
and I never have any regret. Ultimately
this is very much related to motivation.
If I have no negative, selfish motivation,
deep down I will have no guilty feeling.
A second kind of fear is based
on imagination. To overcome that, you
need calmness so that you can
investigate it more closely.
When you look into it in detail,
your imaginary fear
dissipates.

*I*f a person has never encountered love towards himself or herself from any quarter, it is very sad. But if that person can meet even one person who will show unconditional love — simply acceptance and compassion — if he knows that he is an object of someone else's affection and love, it is bound to have an impact, and this will be appreciated. Because there is a seed in himself, this act of love will start to catalyse or ripen that seed.

Crucial to the hermeneutical approach
is the Mahayana principle
of the four reliances.
These are:
(i) reliance on the teaching,
not on the teacher;
(ii) reliance on the meaning, not on
the words that express it;
(iii) reliance on the definitive meaning,
not on the provisional meaning; and
(iv) reliance on the transcendent
wisdom of deep experience,
not on mere knowledge.

*I*n one sense, we can say it is delusion
itself — in the form of the wisdom
derived from delusion — that actually
destroys the delusions. Similarly it is
the blissful experience of emptiness
induced by sexual desire that dissolves
the force of sexual impulses. This is
analogous to the life of wood-born
insects: they consume the very wood
from which they are born. Such
utilization of the path to enlightenment
is a unique feature
of tantra.

I am sometimes asked whether this vow of celibacy is really desirable and indeed whether it is really possible. Suffice to say that its practice is not simply a matter of suppressing sexual desires. On the contrary, it is necessary to fully accept the existence of these desires and to transcend them by the power of reasoning. When successful, the result on the mind can be very beneficial. The trouble with sexual desire is that it is a blind desire and can only ever give temporary satisfaction. Thus, as Nagarjuna said:
'When you have an itch, you scratch. But not to itch at all is better than any amount of scratching.'

*E*ncountering sufferings will definitely
contribute to the elevation of your
spiritual practice, provided you are able
to transform the calamity and
misfortune into the path.

*D*iscipline is a supreme ornament and, whether worn by the old, young or middle-aged, it gives birth only to happiness. It is perfume 'par excellence' and, unlike ordinary perfumes which travel only with the wind, its refreshing aroma travels spontaneously in all directions. A peerless ointment, it brings relief from the hot pains of delusion.

June

When we are able to recognize and forgive ignorant actions done in one's past, we strengthen ourselves and can solve the problems of the present constructively.

*I*t is necessary to have a combination of hearing, thinking and meditation. When you start practising, you should not expect too much. We live in a time of computers and automation, so you may feel that inner development is also an automatic thing for which you press a button and everything changes. It is not so. Inner development is not easy and will take time.

*T*he main cause of depression
is not a lack of material necessities
but a deprivation of the affection of
others.

Anger and hatred cannot bring harmony. The noble task of arms control and disarmament cannot be accomplished by confrontation and condemnation. Hostile attitudes only serve to heat up the situation, whereas a true sense of respect gradually cools down what otherwise could become explosive. We must recognize the frequent contradictions between short-term benefit and long-term harm.

*I*n the meditation of mental
quiescence, in the nine states of mind,
there is a state where striving must be
abandoned; an effortless concentration
is necessary at a certain stage. It is
effortless: that means your mind
becomes very tranquil — with good
qualities and its character complete. At
that moment, if you make an effort that
disturbs the tranquillity. So in order
to maintain that pure tranquillity
effortless effort must be used.

*O*n one occasion I entered
a hospital in Calcutta where they used
huge machines; but they failed in their
diagnosis. Our Tibetan doctors, without
any instruments, touch the wrists,
listen to the various pulses, examine
the person, and know quite precisely
what is wrong. The whole system is
really remarkable.

A very poor, underprivileged person might think that it would be wonderful to have an automobile or a television set, and should he acquire them, at the beginning he would feel very happy. Now if such happiness were something permanent, it would remain forever. But it does not; it goes. After a few months he wants to change the models. The old ones, the same objects, now cause dissatisfaction.

This is the nature of change.

We learn from the principle of
dependent origination that things and
events do not come into being without
causes. Suffering and unsatisfactory
conditions are caused by our own
delusions and the contanimated actions
induced by them.

*D*reams are an idea of the mind.
There are no tangible objects beneath
these sole appearances. Similarly,
self and others, samsara and nirvana,
are designated by the name and the
knowledge about them. Thus,
there is no inherent
existence of any object.

*B*uddhahood is a state free of all
obstructions to knowledge, and
disturbing emotions. It is the state in
which the mind is fully evolved.

Guilt, as experienced in Western culture, is connected with hopelessness and discouragement, and is past-oriented. Genuine remorse, however, is a healthy state of mind — it is future-oriented, connected with hope, and causes us to act, to change.

*T*o study a text, we should take into account the circumstances, the situation, the time, the society and the community where a book was originally written or a teaching taught.

Some people might ask, if everything
is an illusion, what is the use of getting
rid of illusory suffering with an antidote
that is itself illusory? The answer is
that illusory suffering is the result of
causes and conditions that are also
illusory. Even though pain is illusory,
we still suffer from it, and we certainly
do not want it. The same is true of
happiness. It is an illusion, but it is still
something we want. Thus, illusory
antidotes are used to get rid of
illusory sufferings, just like a
magician uses one magical illusion
to counteract another.

What is endeavour? It is finding joy in doing what is good. To do that, it is necessary to remove anything that counteracts it, especially laziness. Related to these is taking undue pleasure in idleness and sleep and being indifferent to samsara as a state of suffering.

*C*loning is an easy, accurate reproduction that implies that we are putting an end to our evolutionary possibilities. We declare that we are perfect, and we stop there. And, on the other hand, if we do attain immortality, that is, if we suppress our death, by the same token we will have to suppress birth, because the earth would become too rapidly overburdened.

One thing can't be doubted, the 'possibility of a quality' is within us. It is called prajna. We can deny everything, except that we have the possibility of being better.
Simply reflect on that.

*I*n the case of animals, usually from the facial expression one can tell what they are going through, whereas human beings are much more sophisticated. To some extent you can feel it, but often they can be deceptive; for instance, initially they are nice but then they turn out to be bad, whereas in the other case, initially they are horrible but then they turn out to be good and reliable.

When we encounter some problem and when someone is about to harm us, then immediately we cultivate anger. Anger comes as a helper or assistant because it makes us bold and courageous and we can retaliate and hit back. When attachment comes, it comes like our best or closest friend. So they are part of our mind, an innate part, and normally we take them for granted and do not bother much about them when they arise within us. Since they come as our friend or helper, therefore, anger and attachment can really deceive us.

Faith dispels doubt and hesitation, it liberates you from suffering and delivers you to the city of peace and happiness. It is faith that removes the mental turbidity and makes your mind clear. Faith reduces your pride and is the root of veneration. It is the supreme lake because you can easily traverse from one stage of the spiritual path to another. It is like your hand which can gather all the virtuous qualities.

*B*uddha has never mentioned that the problems we have encountered are the result of misconstruction of a house or starting a project or work on an inappropriate day or time. Buddha always talked about the negative experiences as a result of having performed negative actions. So, for a good practitioner there is no new year, there is no good day or bad day.

*T*o remain discouraged is not the way
of a human being, we are not birds and
animals, so it is not enough for us to
simply lament and complain but we
should use our intelligence
and work hard.

One aspect of compassion is to respect others' rights and to respect others' views. That is the basis of reconciliation. The human spirit of reconciliation based on compassion is working deep down, whether the person really knows it or not. Our basic human nature is gentleness, therefore, no matter how much we go through violence and other bad things, ultimately the proper solution is to return to human feeling and affection. So, affection or compassion is not only a religious matter, but in our day-to-day life it is quite indispensable.

As far as your personal requirements
are concerned, the ideal is to have fewer
involvements, fewer obligations and
fewer affairs, business, or whatever.
However, so far as the interest of the
larger community is concerned, you
must have as many involvements as
possible and as many activities
as possible.

Within oneself, within each single
person, one finds many inconsistencies
and contradictions. Sometimes the
disparity between one's thoughts
early and late in the day is so great
that one spends all one's energy
trying to figure out how
it can be resolved. This can
lead to headaches. So naturally,
between two persons, between
parents and children, between brothers
and sisters, there are differences.
Conflicts and disagreements
are bound to happen.
If so, then how do we
deal with them? If we have
confidence in our capacity for
reconciliation then we will
be able to deal with
these situations.

When we talk of the six perfections —
generosity, ethical discipline, patience,
perseverance, concentration and
wisdom — they can also be found in
other, non-bodhisattva practitioners
who are working more towards their
own individual liberation. What makes
the practice of these six factors
perfect is the motivation involved.
In order for one's practice
of patience to be a practice
of the perfection of patience,
you need the motivation which is
bodhicitta. If your practice is
motivated by bodhicitta — the
aspiration to attain enlightenment
for the benefit of all —
then your practice becomes
truly a practice of perfection.

*T*ime never waits
but keeps flowing. Not only
does time flow unhindered, but
correspondingly our life too
keeps moving onward all the time.
If something goes wrong,
we cannot turn back time
and try again. In that sense,
there is no genuine
second chance.

A single word or expression in tantra
can have four different meanings
corresponding to the four levels
of interpretation, known as the four
modes of understanding,
which are: (i) the literal meaning;
(ii) the general meaning; (iii) the hidden
meaning; and (iv) the ultimate meaning.

I don't have any experience in applying
Western psychotherapy to the Buddhist
path. I do know, however, that
intimacy is necessary for a spiritual
practitioner, especially if that
individual is trying to overcome his
mental problems. When you open
yourself up mentally, you do so
only with someone you trust from the
bottom of your heart, someone you feel
very close to. To open yourself
up in this way is an
important step in overcoming
mental problems.

*T*he earth is, to a certain extent, our mother. She is so kind, because whatever we do, she tolerates it. But now, the time has come when our power to destroy is so extreme that mother earth is compelled to tell us to be careful. The population explosion and many other indicators make that clear, don't they? Nature has its own natural limitations.

*T*ranquil or calm abiding is a heightened state of awareness possessing a very single-pointed nature, accompanied by faculties of mental and physical suppleness. Your body and mind become especially flexible, receptive and serviceable. Special insight is a heightened state of awareness, also accompanied by mental and physical suppleness, in which your faculty of analysis is immensely advanced. Thus calm abiding is absorptive in nature, whereas special insight is analytic in nature.

July

*P*eace is of little value to someone who is dying of hunger or cold. It will not remove the pain of torture inflicted on a prisoner of conscience. It does not comfort those who have lost their loved ones in floods caused by senseless deforestation in a neighbouring country. Peace can only last where human rights are respected, where the people are fed, and where individuals and nations are free. True peace with ourselves and with the world around us can only be achieved through the development of mental peace.

*F*irst we must help; then, later we can talk about the causes of any tragedy. There is an Indian saying: if you are struck by a poisonous arrow, it is important first to pull it out; there is no time to ask who shot it, what sort of poison it is, and so on. First handle the immediate problem, and later investigate. Similarly, when we encounter human suffering, it is important to respond with compassion rather than to question the politics of those we help.

*D*ue to karmic influences, the world appears in different ways to certain people. Like when a human being, a god and a *preta*—three sentient beings—look at one bowl of water, the karmic factors make the human being see it as water, while the god sees nectar and the *preta* sees blood. The same object, due to special forces of Karma, appears differently to each of them.

*I*n the correlation between ethics and politics, should deep moral convictions form the guideline for the political practitioner, man and his society will reap far-reaching benefits. It is an absurd assumption that religion and morality have no place in politics and that a man of religion should seclude himself as a hermit.

I believe in justice and in human determination. In the history of man it has already been proved that the human will is more powerful than the gun. So although for us this is the toughest period, I quite firmly believe that the Tibetan people, their culture, and the Tibetan faith will survive, will flourish once again.

*H*uman relations based on
mutual compassion and love are
fundamentally important to
human happiness.

*R*ather than being unhappy and
hateful, we should rejoice in the success
of others.

*U*nlike an external enemy, the inner enemy cannot regroup and launch a comeback once it has been destroyed from within.

There are many circumstances that make us unjust, ambitious or aggressive. All around us, everything is pushing us in that direction, often out of some commercial interest: I have to possess this or that object, otherwise my life will be lamentable. The world is presented to us as essentially competitive, divided into 'the winners' and 'the losers', but that too is a false vision, deliberately false. It is a rapid scan of the surface which eliminates any descent into the self, any meditation and reflection.

*T*he power of media, whether direct
or indirect, is a real power which
acts on us, which modifies our
behaviour, our tastes and probably
our thoughts. Like all authority,
it cannot be applied at random.
Otherwise, that power
could become arbitrary and
irresponsible. The power gives
mediamen responsibility comparable
to religious or political responsibility.
In their own way they contribute
to the establishment and
maintenance of a human community.
The well-being of that community
should be their first concern.

*T*he training of the mind is an art. If
this can be considered as art, one's life
is art. I am not interested in the
physical aspect of art. I simply meditate
and train my mind. And as far as
external appearance is concerned,
nature in its pristine form
is also art.

*I*f you rely on someone who has
lower qualities than yourself, that will
lead to your degeneration;
if you rely on someone who has
qualities similar to yourself,
you will stay where you are;
and if you rely on someone who has
better qualities than yourself, that will
help you to achieve sublime status.

I sometimes think that the act of
bringing food is one of the basic roots of
all relationships.

*I*f students sincerely point out
the faults of the guru and explain any
contradictory behaviour, this will,
in fact, help the guru to correct
that behaviour and adjust
any wrong actions.

*F*or a meditator who has a certain
degree of inner stability and realization,
every experience comes as a teaching;
every event, every experience one is
exposed to comes as a kind of
learning experience.

When a problem first arises,
try to remain humble, maintain
a sincere attitude, and be concerned
that the outcome is fair.
Of course, others may try to
take advantage of you, and
if your remaining detached
only encourages unjust aggression,
adopt a strong stand. This,
however, should be done with
compassion, and if it is necessary
to express your views and
take strong countermeasures,
do so without anger or ill-intent.

*T*here are different types of
attachment in relation to different
objects: attachment toward form,
appearance, sound, smell, tactile
sensations, and so on. All of these
individually are powerful enough to
cause a lot of problems and
difficulties. However, the strongest
form of attachment seems to be
sexual attachment. Here we find
attachment toward all the five senses
involved. Therefore, it is all the
more powerful and has the potential
for problems and destruction.

Should we persist in our normal self-centred tendencies and behaviour in spite of our human birth, we would be wasting a great opportunity. Our tenure in this world should not be that of a troublemaker in the human community.

Great compassion and wisdom are the chief qualities of the Buddha. Even in worldly terms, the more intelligent and knowledgeable a person is, the more the person commands respect. Similarly, the more compassionate, kind and gentle a person, the more he or she should be respected. So if you are able to develop that intelligence and altruism to their fullest extent, then you are truly admirable and deserve to be respected.

*D*elusion is a state of mind that is
very obvious: when it arises within
the mind it causes mental disturbances
and anxieties in the individual.
Furthermore, it causes many problems
and difficulties in society, often on a
national scale. Right from the beginning
of human civilization, delusions have
been the real causes of problems,
trouble and conflict within society.
It is delusion that forces one
to be attracted and attached to
one's own side and to feel hatred
and anger towards the opposite side.
Thus, one creates many divisions
within the human community.
All of these come about through
the underlying force of the
attachment to one's own self.

*I*n the present circumstances,
no one can afford to assume that
someone else will solve their problems.
Every individual has a responsibility to
help guide our global family in the right
direction. Good wishes are not
sufficient; we must become
actively engaged.

*I*n the case of making bombs, the people involved are specialists. They are focussing on something very narrow and becoming extremely expert in that area, without seeing the broader consequences of their acts. It is a kind of tunnel vision. As long as they focus on that, the self-deception is supported. From the exploitist's viewpoint, this is a great achievement. In their own right, in their own domain, they are doing something extraordinary.

The guru, the spiritual teacher,
is responsible for his or her
improper behaviour. It is the student's
responsibility not to be drawn into it.
The blame is on both. Partly it is
because the student is too obedient
and devoted to the spiritual master,
a kind of blind acceptance of that
person's guidance. This always spoils
the person. But of course part of
the blame lies with the spiritual
master, because he lacks the integrity
that is necessary to be immune
to that kind of vulnerability.

When through rituals and formalities
you create the spiritual space and
atmosphere that you are seeking,
then the process will have a powerful
effect on your experience. When you lack
the inner dimension for that spiritual
experience you are aspiring to,
then rituals become mere formalities,
external elaborations. In that case,
clearly, they lose their meaning
and become unnecessary customs —
just a good excuse for passing time.

Sexual misconduct has negative spiritual and social consequences. It causes disharmony between life partners and has an adverse effect upon their children. Rape is worse, harming another's body by force, leading justifiably to controversies in courts of law and multiplying social problems.

When others insult, rebuke and speak unpleasant words to us, although an intolerable pain arises like a thorn at the heart, if we comprehend the teachings then we can recognize the essenceless nature of these words which resemble an echo. So, just as when an inanimate object is scolded, we will experience not the slightest mental turmoil.

*T*oday we face a number of problems. Some are natural calamities, which we must accept and face as best as we can. But some others are man-made problems created by our own misbehaviour and bad thoughts which can be avoided. One such problem arises from ideological or even religious conflicts when men fight each other, losing sight of human ends or goals. All different faiths and systems are only methods to achieve a goal which for the average person is happiness in life. Therefore, at no time should we place means above ends: the supremacy of man over matter and all that it entails must be maintained at all times.

*T*he fact remains that the birth-cycles of all sentient beings are beginningless, and that numberless times in previous lives we have each fulfilled the role of a mother. The feeling of a mother for her child is a classic example of love. For the safety, protection and welfare of her children, a mother is ready to sacrifice her very life. Recognizing this, children should be grateful to their mothers and express their gratitude by performing virtuous deeds.

*O*ne of the charactcristics of karmic
theory is that there is a definite,
commensurate relationship between
cause and effect. There is no way that
negative actions or unwholesome deeds
can result in joy and happiness. Joy and
happiness, by definition, are the results
or fruits of wholesome actions. So, from
that point of view, it is possible for us to
admire not so much the immediate
action, but the real causes of joy.

*T*here is said to be a relationship between dreaming, on the one hand, and the gross and subtle levels of the body on the other. But it's also said there is such a thing as a 'special dream state'. In that state, the 'special dream body' is created from the mind and from vital energy within the body. This special dream body is able to dissociate entirely from the gross physical body and travel elsewhere. One way of developing this special dream body is first of all to recognize the dream as a dream when it is over. Then, you find that the dream is malleable, and you can make efforts to gain control over it.

*R*egarding my actual daily practice, I spend, at the very least, five and a half hours per day in prayer, meditation and study. On top of this, I also pray whenever I can during odd moments of the day, for example over meals and while travelling. In this last case, I have three main reasons for doing so: firstly, it contributes towards fulfilment of my daily duty; secondly, it helps to pass the time productively; thirdly, it assuages fear! More seriously though, I see no distinction between religious practice and daily life.

August

When we practice, initially,
as a basis we control ourselves,
stopping the bad actions which
hurt others as much as
we can. This is defensive. After that,
when we develop certain qualifications,
then as an active goal we should help
others. In the first stage, sometimes
we need isolation; however, after you
have some confidence, some strength,
you must remain in contact with society,
and serve it in any field —
health, education, politics, or whatever.
In order to serve you must remain
in society.

According to its level of subtlety,
consciousness is classified into three
levels: the waking state or gross level
of consciousness; the consciousness of
the dream state which is more subtle;
and the consciousness during sleep,
dreamless sleep, which is subtler still.
Similarly, the three stages of birth,
death and the intermediate state
are also established in terms of the
subtlety of their levels of consciousness.
Upon the basis of the continuity of
the stream of consciousness
is established the existence of
rebirth and reincarnation.

We must each lead a way of life
with self-awareness and compassion,
to do as much as we can.
Then, whatever happens, we will
have no regrets.

We can speak of
an effect and a cause on both,
the disturbing side and the
liberating side. The true sufferings
and true causes of sufferings
are the effect and cause on
the side of things that
we do not want;
the true cessation and
the true paths are
the effect and cause
on the side of things
that we desire.

Vegetarianism is very admirable. However, according to Buddhism, there is no unequivocal prohibition against eating meat. What is specifically prohibited is taking any meat that you have ordered with the knowledge, or even the suspicion, that it has been killed especially for you.

When receiving the teachings, it is important to have the correct attitude. It is not practising the Dharma properly to listen with the intention of gaining material advantage or reputation. Neither should our goal be higher rebirth in the next life, nor should we be wishing only for our own liberation from samsara. These are all attitudes we should reject. Instead, let us listen to the teachings with the determined wish to attain the state of omniscience for the sake of all beings.

*I*n Tibetan, the word for blessing means transformation through majesty or power. In short, the meaning of blessing is to bring about, as a result of the experience, a transformation in one's mind for the better.

*T*he truth of suffering
is that we experience many
different types of suffering.
The three categories are: suffering of
suffering — this refers to things such as
headaches; suffering of change — this is
related to the feeling of restlessness
after being comfortable;
and all-pervasive suffering that
acts as the basis of the first two
categories and is
under the control of Karma
and the disturbing mind.

*T*he criterion that distinguishes
a school as Buddhist is its acceptance
of four fundamental tenets, known as
the four seals. These are: (i) all composite
phenomena are impermanent;
(ii) all contaminated things and events are
unsatisfactory; (iii) all phenomena are
empty and selfless; and (iv) nirvana is
true peace.

True practitioners are unaffected by external pressures and their own emotions, they are free to secure the temporary and ultimate benefit of both themselves and others. They remain independent, fear nothing, and are never at odds with themselves. Always peaceful, they are friendly with all, and everything they say is helpful. Wherever we go, let us be humble and avoid being noisy or bossy. Let us not hurt other people's feelings or cause them to act negatively.

When things are not going well for someone we dislike, what is the point in rejoicing? It does not make his present suffering any worse and even if it did, how sad it would be that we should wish such a thing.

*O*ur whole educational system is in a crisis. It can't adapt. In fact, this crisis extends to industry and politics. Everything seems to be escaping our thought, and hence our control.

*I*t seems to me that God has fallen asleep somewhere. I was joking, as you might imagine, since we make no allowance for a creator god. But it is true that if God has fallen asleep, then it is our job to wake Him up. One can't blame all our troubles on God. Nor on destiny, nor on Karma, which is our law of the chain of causes, of deeds and effects. All this comes from a rather cowardly attitude.

I am absolutely opposed to death penalty. My predecessor abolished it in Tibet. Today I find it unbelievable that it persists in large countries like China and India. In the name of justice they are still killing people in the country of Mahatma Gandhi! In the very land where the Buddha taught! The death penalty is pure violence, a barbaric and useless violence. Dangerous even, because it can only lead to other acts of violence — as all violence does. The supreme punishment ought to be a life sentence and without brutality.

*I*t is difficult to impose censorship in a democracy. Though we can still see censorship at work in India, real violence and even explicit eroticism are permitted in Indian films. Women can display themselves very provocatively, as they do everywhere else. Yet until recently men and women never kissed on the lips. People killed one another, but they didn't kiss. And yet it is more agreeable to kiss than to kill! In Indian films, most of the time we witness the development of a love story, which meets violent opposition, but in the end the good-hearted people are reunited and rewarded, while the villains are punished.

*I*n the cycle of rebirths, which we call samsara, from time to time there occurs the phenomenon of reincarnation. First of all, let us make a distinction. The cycle of rebirths — samsara — is the very condition of all life. No existence escapes it, unless it gets to nirvana. This condition is painful, because it obliges us to live and live again, on levels that can be worse than those we have known. If rebirth is an obligation, reincarnation is a choice. It is the power granted to certain worthy individuals to control their future birth.

Guilt, according to some scholars, is something that can be overcome. It does not exist in Buddhist terminology. With the Buddha nature all negative things can be purified. Guilt is incompatible with our thinking as you are part of an action but not fully responsible for it. You are just part of the contributing factor. However, in some cases one must repent, deliberately hold responsibility, have regret and never commit the mistake again.

As a result of long study and understanding if you get proud and haughty, it is very unfortunate. If we see pride among people who have no idea about Dharma practice, it is understandable. However, if afflictive emotions and haughtiness are present among Dharma practitioners, it is a great disgrace to the practice.

*T*he advantage of relying on a spiritual teacher is that if you have accumulated an action that would project you into a negative state of existence, the result of that could be experienced just in this life in the form of minor sufferings or minor problems, or even experiencing the result in a dream and through that way one could destroy the destructive result of negative actions.

*I*n the case of the death of a person who has been engaging in non-virtuous practices, the consciousness would start dissolving from the upper part of the body and withdraw within the heart. In case of a person who has performed virtuous activities, the dissolution of the heat starts from the lower part of the body and finally withdraws at the heart. In both cases the transference of consciousness would take place at the centre.

One should enter or do spiritual
practice with a motivation similar to
the motivation and attitude of a child
that is fully absorbed in sports or play.
A child fully engrossed in play gets so
delighted with it that the child never
feels satisfied — such should be your
mental attitude in making effort
in Dharma practice.

*T*here are many afflictive emotions
such as conceit, arrogance, jealousy,
desire, lust, closed-mindedness, and so
on, but of all these, hatred or anger is
singled out as the greatest evil. This is
done for two reasons. One is that hatred
or anger is the greatest stumbling block
for a practitioner who is aspiring to
enhance his or her altruism and attain
a good heart. Second, when hatred or
anger are generated they have the
capacity to destroy one's virtue and
calmness of mind.

*I*t is possible to indicate one's particular spiritual way of life through external means, such as wearing certain clothes, having a shrine or altar in one's house, doing recitations and chanting. However, these practices are secondary to one's religious or spiritual way of life because all of these activities can be performed by a person who harbours a very negative state of mind. On the other hand, all the virtues of mind, the mental qualities, are genuine spiritual qualities because all of these internal mental qualities cannot exist in a single moment simultaneously with ill feelings or negative states of mind.

Regarding inter-gender relationships, I see two principal types of relationships based on sexual attraction. One form is pure sexual desire in which the motive or impetus is temporary satisfaction, a sort of immediate gratification. But it is not very reliable or stable because the individuals are relating to each other not as people, but rather as objects. In the second type, attraction is not predominantly physical. Rather, there is an underlying respect and appreciation of the value of the other person, based on one's feeling that the other person is kind, nice and gentle. One can therefore accord respect and dignity to that other individual.

While one possesses the facilities of wealth, position, education, and so on, it is crucial that there be some internal restraining factor that constantly keeps one in check so one is not spoiled by these facilities and never loses the fundamental insight into the underlying unsatisfactory nature of cyclic existence. The proper perspective is to utilize this as an aid in the path and for working for the benefit of other sentient beings. There is always the need to maintain balance, not to go to any extremes, and to have full knowledge of how to proceed along the path in the best and most effective way.

*T*here are three types of joyous effort :
(i) armour-like joyous effort;
(ii) joyous effort in gathering virtues; and
(iii) joyous effort in working for others.
The main obstacles to the development of
these efforts are the different levels of
laziness — primarily the laziness of
procrastination, and the laziness
stemming from indolence and from a
sense of inferiority.

*I*n addition to practising during the waking state, if you can also use your consciousness during sleep for wholesome purposes, then the power of your spiritual practice will be all the greater. Otherwise at least a few hours each night will be just a waste. So if you can transform your sleep into something virtuous, this is useful. The Sutrayana method is to try as you go to sleep to develop a wholesome mental state, such as compassion, or the visualization of impermanence or emptiness.

The creatures that inhabit this earth — be they human beings or animals — are here to contribute, each in its own particular way, to the beauty and prosperity of the world. Many creatures have toiled singly or jointly to make our lives comfortable. The food we eat, the clothes we wear, have not just dropped from the sky. Many creatures have laboured to produce them. That is why we should be grateful to all our fellow creatures. Compassion and loving kindness are the hallmarks of achievement and happiness.

*O*verall I have found much that is impressive about Western society. In particular, I admire its energy and creativity and hunger for knowledge. On the other hand, a number of things about the Western way of life cause me concern. People there have an inclination to think in terms of 'black and white' and 'either, or', which ignores the facts of interdependence and relativity. Between two points of view they tend to lose sight of the grey areas. Also, with thousands of brothers and sisters for neighbours, so many people appear to be able to show their true feelings only to their cats and dogs.

*B*lessings are not enough. Blessings must come from within. Without your own effort, it is impossible for blessings to come.

A skilled physician ministers to his patients individually, giving each the appropriate medicine necessary to cure his particular disease. Furthermore, the method and materials of treatment will vary according to the particular combination of circumstances of time and country. Yet all the widely differing medicines and medical methods are similar in that each of them aims to deliver the suffering patient from his sickness. In the same way, all religious teachings and methods are intended to free living beings from misery and the cause of misery, and to provide them with happiness and the cause of happiness.

September

*T*he task of man is to help others; that's my firm teaching, that's my message. That is my own belief. For me, the fundamental question is better relations, better relations among human beings — and whatever I can contribute to that.

One great question underlies our experience, whether we think about it consciously or not: what is the purpose of life? From the moment of birth, every human being wants happiness and does not want suffering. Neither social conditioning nor education nor ideology affect this. From the very core of our being, we simply desire contentment. Therefore, it is important to discover what will bring about the greatest degree of happiness.

A limit to the size of the family is desirable. We have to take care of birth control. It is very, very essential to have less children, and those children must be properly taken care of. Besides education, one must introduce to them the reverence for life and the value of human affection.

*T*o overcome attachment we should meditate on the ugliness of what attracts us. The antidote to pride is meditation on the aggregates. To counteract ignorance we should concentrate on the movement of the breath and on interdependence. The root of the mind's turmoil is, in fact, ignorance on account of which we fail to understand the true nature of things. The mind is brought under control by purifying our mistaken notion of reality.

*T*he three physical non-virtues are:
killing, stealing and sexual misconduct.
The four verbal non-virtues are: lying,
divisiveness, harsh speech and
senseless speech.
The three mental non-virtues are:
covetousness, harmful intent
and wrong view.

*P*erhaps in monasteries in the West there is leisure, but outside — especially in the cities — life seems to be running at a rapid pace, like a clock, never stopping for an instant! So, if you look at life in an urban community, it seems as if every aspect of a person's life has to be so precise, designed like a screw that has to fit exactly in the hole. In some sense, you have no control over your own life. In order to survive, you have to follow this pattern and the pace that is set for you.

*J*ust like the earth, may I support
beings as numerous as the sky is vast.
And as long as they have not attained
enlightenment, may I devote myself
entirely to their happiness.

When people get angry they lose all sense of happiness. Even if they are good-looking and normally peaceful, their faces turn livid and ugly. Anger upsets their physical well-being and disturbs their rest; it destroys their appetites and makes them age prematurely. Happiness, peace and sleep evade them, and they no longer appreciate people who have helped them and deserve their trust and gratitude.

*L*eaving aside memory — which allows us to remember, for example, the experiences of our youth — we all have latent and unconscious tendencies that arise under certain circumstances and influence the way our minds react. Such tendencies are the product of powerful experiences in the recent or distant past, which cause us to react unconsciously without our necessarily remembering those experiences. It is difficult to explain these tendencies and how they manifest other than by saying that they are the imprints of past experiences on the subtle consciousness.

*T*he growth in population is very much bound up with poverty, and in turn poverty plunders the earth. When human groups are dying of hunger, they eat everything, grass, insects, everything. They cut down the trees, they leave the land dry and bare. All other concerns vanish. That's why in the next thirty years the problems we call 'environmental' will be the hardest that humanity has to face.

Since we have a natural compassion in us, and that compassion has to manifest itself, it might be good to awaken it. Violence done to an innocent person, for example, can make us indignant, scandalize us, and in so doing help us to discover our compassion. By its very violence television might keep us in a state of alert. However, it is very dangerous if violence leads to indifference. Thus, a central point of our teaching is: how to reach non-attachment without falling into indifference.

A real 'Tibethood' was born from the difficult passage in the long history of Tibet. Centuries and centuries of rootedness can make you forget that feeling. The bonds with the earth seem secure, untouchable. Then something unexpected happens that calls those bonds into question. You discover a cynical brutality, the crushing use of force, your own weakness. Finally you leave, you never see your country except from far away. It gets ravaged, occupied, and still you realize that it hasn't disappeared, that it subsists in you, that you still feel Tibetan. Then you begin to wonder, what does being Tibetan mean?

We are afraid to die because we don't know the day nor the hour, because death can surprise us at any moment. Because we fear what comes after death, we are afraid of finding ourselves in an unknown and disagreeable place, filled with anxiety. If we want to die well, we must learn to live well. The experience of death is extremely important, because our state of mind at that moment can decide the quality of our future rebirth. We can even, at the moment of dying, make a special effort. In the course of it meditation can reach an unequalled summit, as shown by the preservation of the body.

*J*ust as rust, which arose from the iron itself, wears out the iron, likewise, performing an action without examination would destroy us by projecting us into a negative state of existence.

As students, you should first watch and investigate thoroughly. Do not consider someone as a teacher or guru until you have certain confidence in the person's integrity. This is very important. Even after that, if some unhealthy things happen, you have the liberty to reject them. Students should make sure that they don't spoil the guru.

*T*here are three types of wisdom, or
three stages in one's understanding.
First is the stage of hearing or learning,
the initial stage when you read or hear
about something. The second stage is
when, after learning, you think about
the issue or the topic constantly, and
through constant familiarity and
thinking, your understanding becomes
clearer. Then at that time you begin to
have certain feelings or experiences.
This third stage is called 'meditatively
acquired wisdom'. This is when you not
only intellectually understand the
subject matter but also, through
meditative experience, are able to feel it.

*I*t is vital for a leader to keep in touch
with the common people. I myself had
learned at an early age that anyone
who wishes to lead must remain close to
the common people.

*O*ur judgements, even concerning ordinary things, are frequently clouded by our emotions. For example, we often see the actions of our loved ones — even if they are harmful — as wonderful, whereas we judge even the positive actions of a person we dislike as pretentious and false. We cannot rely upon our perceptions; it is a fact that we misapprehend many situations. If this is a general fact, how can we still stubbornly maintain that our perceptions about our own spiritual masters must be true?

*H*uman beings are social animals who depend for their survival on others' cooperation and assistance. So it is better not to have a companion at all than to have one who is very aggressive and harmful. You can never rely on such a person but always have to be suspicious and apprehensive about him or her. And conversely, if your own character and personality is such that all people avoid you, that is very sad. Therefore, a kind heart and compassion are the real sources of peace and happiness.

Whether their entire life will be successful or not depends much upon the atmosphere young children feel throughout the day. In a family where there is love and compassion, the children will become happier and more successful human beings. Without love, there is a danger of spoiling or ruining their whole life. Human affection is thus most influential for children's development.

Western brains work, they work a great deal, but always in the direction of efficiency. In that way the mind puts itself at the service of the result. Like all servants, it renounces its independence. I am talking about another form of spiritual life, more detached and deeper, free from the obsession of a goal to be reached. In a way, the universal invasion of technology, everywhere it goes, lessens the life of the mind.

*I*f you are the sort of person who always speaks nicely in front of others but says nasty things about them behind their backs, of course nobody will like you.

*T*here is no way to escape death, it is just like trying to escape when you are surrounded by four great mountains touching the sky. There is no escape from these four mountains of birth, old age, sickness and death. Ageing destroys youth, sickness destroys health, degeneration of life destroys all excellent qualities and death destroys life. Even if you are a great runner, you cannot run away from death. You cannot stop death with your wealth, through your magic performances or recitation of mantras or even medicines. Therefore, it is wise to prepare for your death.

There is a true feminist movement in Buddhism that relates to the goddess Tara. Following her cultivation of bodhicitta, the bodhisattva's motivation, she looked upon those striving towards full awakening and she felt that there were too few people who attained Buddhahood as women. So she vowed, 'I have developed bodhicitta as a woman. For all of my lifetimes along the path I vow to be born as a woman, and in my final lifetime when I attain Buddhahood, then, too, I will be a woman.'

*A*nything that contradicts
experience and logic
should be abandoned.

*T*he metaphor of light is a common image in all the major religious traditions. In the Buddhist context, light is particularly associated with wisdom and knowledge; darkness is associated with ignorance and a state of mis-knowledge. This corresponds to the two aspects of the path: there is the method aspect, which includes such practices as compassion and tolerance, and the wisdom or knowledge aspect, the insight penetrating the nature of reality. It is the knowledge or wisdom aspect of the path that is the true antidote to dispelling ignorance.

We do not regard a person as an authority simply on the basis of their fame, position, power, good looks, wealth and so on, but rather because we find what they say on issues related to their particular field of expertise convincing and reliable. In brief, we do not generally take a person to be an authority on a subject simply out of respect and admiration for them as a person. Similarly, when we take the Buddha as an authority, as a reliable teacher, we do so on the basis of having investigated and examined his principal teaching, the Four Noble Truths.

I am talking to you and you are listening to me. We are generally under the impression that there is a speaker and an audience and there is the sound of words being spoken but, in ultimate truth, if I search within myself I will not find the words, and if you search yourselves you will not find them — they are all void like empty space. Yet they are not completely non-existent. They must exist, for we are able to feel them. What I am saying is being heard by you, and you are in turn thinking on the subject. My speech is producing some effect, yet if we search for them we cannot find them. This mystery relates to the dual nature of truth.

I find that giving a discourse based on
religious texts is a good way of showing
that religion has a lot to tell us, no
matter what situation we find ourselves
in. However, I am better at it now than
I was in the beginning. In those days I
lacked confidence, although it improved
every time I spoke in public. Also, I
found, as every teacher does, that there
is nothing like teaching to
help one learn.

*O*ur experience is based on the five inner and five outer elements. When your meditative experience gets deep enough to control the five inner elements, then there is the possibility of controlling the five outer elements. Although space seems empty, once you develop the energies, you can control it. When that happens, you can look right through solid things and walk in empty space as if it were solid.

October

Man and society are interdependent, hence the quality of man's behaviour as an individual and as a participant in his society is inseparable. Reparations have been attempted in the past in order to lessen the malaise and dysfunctional attitudes of our social world, in order to build a society which is more just and equal. Institutions and organizations have been established with their charters of noble ideology to combat these social problems. For all intents and purposes, the objectives have been laudable; but it has been unfortunate that basically good ideas have been defeated by man's inherent self-interest.

An area in Tibetan Buddhism which
may be of interest to scientists is the
relationship between the physical
elements and the nerves, in particular
the relationship between the elements
in the brain and consciousness.
Involved here are the changes in
consciousness, happy or unhappy states
of mind etc., the kind of effect they have
on the elements within the brain, and
the consequent effect that it has on the
body. Certain physical illnesses, for
example, improve or worsen according
to the state of mind.

All the waters and rivers of different lands and climes have their ultimate meeting point in the ocean. So, too, the differing viewpoints on society, the variety of economic theories and the means to their attainment benefit mankind itself. There is no point in indulging in dissension-creating discussions on differing ideologies. No positive result has accrued from attempting to convert all men of different temperaments and likings into one common ideology and mode of behaviour. This can clearly be seen from the contemporary history of both the East and the West.

Make efforts to consider
as transitory all adverse
circumstances and disturbances.
Like ripples in a pool, they occur and
soon disappear. Insofar as
our lives are karmically conditioned,
they are characterized by
endless cycles of problems.
One problem appears and
passes, and soon
another one begins.

*B*uddha advises:
'O bhikshus and wise men,
just as a goldsmith would test his gold
by burning, cutting and rubbing it,
so must you examine my words
and accept them
but not merely out of
reverence for me.'

Wise parents,
without any anger,
may sometimes scold
or even punish their children.
This is permissible, but
if you really get angry
and whack the child
too much, then you yourself
will feel regret
in the future. However, with
a good motivation of
seeking a child's welfare,
it is possible to
display an expression
appropriate to what
the child needs
at that moment.

*T*he ignorance, arrogance and
obstinacy of certain individuals,
whether their intentions were good or
evil, have been at the root of
all the tragedies of history. The mere
names of these ruthless tyrants inspire
fear and loathing. So the extent to
which people will like us naturally
depends on how much, or how little we
think of others' good.

*E*xile has helped me. When, at some
point in our lives, we meet a real
tragedy — which could happen to any
one of us — we can react in two ways.
Obviously, we can lose hope, let
ourselves slip into discouragement, into
alcohol, drugs and unending sadness.
Or else, we can wake ourselves up,
discover in ourselves an energy that
was hidden there, and act with more
clarity, more force.

*T*he void, shunyata, among the four fundamental Buddhist notions (the three others being impermanence, interdependence and suffering) is certainly the most mysterious and hard to grasp. What is this immense edifice of experience and thought that in the end only opens up on an absence of substance? What would be the foundation of that edifice and of the mind that built it? If the void is the only reality that isn't illusory, who escapes the net of all maya? Who has cast this net? Can one live over a dizzying void? Can we imagine a dream without a dreamer? The void is a scientific notion. We are empty, the matter that composes us is, so to speak, empty.

Another issue which is very dear to my vision of the future is global demilitarization. This may sound idealistic to many people. I am aware that implementing it requires a step-by-step approach that will entail a process of re-thinking in policy and public education. The first step towards this goal is an international ban on the arms trade and an expansion of demilitarized zones in all parts of the world. Recent progress on dismantling nuclear arsenals and nuclear test bans represent an encouraging and significant beginning.

*I*n the case of a small child, the child has to grow up into a well-built young man but the growth takes place with the passage of time. It cannot happen overnight. Likewise the transformation of mind will also take time. Nowadays in many places, by using certain injections, pigs, cows and birds suddenly grow. Then they are killed and consumed. This negative practice also has an effect on human beings. So, when we talk of spiritual practice, we cannot inject certain qualities and suddenly transform the mind.

*I*n the beginning of Buddhist practice, our ability to serve others is limited. The emphasis is on healing ourselves, transforming our minds and hearts. But as we continue, we become stronger and increasingly able to serve others. But until then, we may get overwhelmed by the sufferings and difficulties of other people. We may become exhausted and not be able to serve others effectively, not to mention ourselves. It is natural to feel some limitation with both, and we just have to accept that.

When one is in an intense state of hatred, even a very close friend appears somehow 'frosty', cold and distant, or quite annoying. If one harbours hateful thoughts, it ruins one's health. Even if one has wonderful possessions, in the moment of anger one feels like throwing them or breaking them. So there is no guarantee that wealth alone can give one the joy or fulfilment that one seeks.

*I*n Buddha's time there was a king who committed the heinous crime of murdering his father. But he was totally overwhelmed by his crime, and depressed. When Buddha visited him he made a statement that parents are to be killed, but he didn't mean it literally. Buddha was using parents as a kind of metaphor for desire and attachment that lead to rebirth. Because Karma and desire combine to create rebirth, in some sense they are like parents. Thus, he meant that Karma and desire are to be eliminated.

When one meditates on mindfulness of the body, reflecting upon the manner in which the body comes into being, and examining the causal conditions, then one will also see the impurities of the body. Then, from that perspective, one will find that even those who seem successful in worldly terms are not really objects worthy of envy; they are still within the bondage of suffering and dissatisfaction. The greater the success one enjoys in worldly terms, the more complex the psychological make-up seems to be, because there is a much more complex nexus of hopes and fears, apprehensions and inhibitions.

*N*egative actions have the potential to increase, whereas positive actions can be destroyed by many adverse circumstances.

*T*here is no possibility of happiness and peace while someone is under the leadership of a very negative person. Therefore, reflect upon the fact that you are under the rule of ignorance; ignorance is like a despotic king, and anger and attachment are like his ministers. We live under the tyranny and influence of ignorance, the self-grasping attitude, and also the self-cherishing attitude — factors that all the buddhas and bodhisattvas treat as real enemies.

*T*here are different types of patience: the patience of being indifferent to the harm inflicted by others, the patience of voluntarily accepting hardship, and the patience developed through reasoned conviction in the Dharma.

*O*nly a spontaneous feeling of empathy with others can really inspire us to act on their behalf. Nevertheless, compassion does not arise mechanically. Such a sincere feeling must grow gradually, cultivated within each individual, based on their own conviction of its worth. Adopting a kind attitude thus becomes a personal matter. How each of us behave in daily life is, after all, the real test of compassion.

I feel there is a difference between the mental conflicts that one feels and the emotions they give rise to — anger, hostility and so forth. If you are not able to express the mental conflicts that you have — then at a later point of your life, when you are able to express these mental conflicts, they are automatically accompanied by hostility and anger. Therefore, it is important to express one's suffering, not so much the hostility, but rather the suffering.

Great vigilance must be maintained at all times when dealing in areas about which we do not have great understanding. This, of course, is where science can help. We consider things to be mysterious only when we do not understand them. I realize that results of enquiries are dependent on the experiments employed to achieve them. However, not finding something does not mean that it does not exist. It only proves that the experiment was incapable of finding it. It is also important to keep in mind the limitations imposed by nature itself.

*I*f any sensible person thinks deeply,
he will respect justice. There is an
inborn appreciation and respect for
justice within our human body.
In children, we find what is natural
to the human character. But as they
grow up, they develop a lot of
conditioning and wrong attitudes.
I often feel there is more truthfulness
in a small child and I find many
reasons to have confidence in
human courage and human nature.

What is reborn are our habits.
Enlightenment is the ending of rebirth,
which means a complete
non-attachment or non-identification
with all thoughts, feelings, perceptions,
physical sensations and ideas.

We speak of three different types of faith. The first is faith in the form of admiration that you have toward a particular person or a particular state of being. The second is aspiring faith. There is a sense of emulation — you aspire to attain that state of being. The third type is the faith of conviction.

As a spiritual trainee, you must be prepared to endure the hardships involved in a genuine spiritual pursuit and be determined to sustain your effort and will. You must anticipate the multiple obstacles that you are bound to encounter along the path and understand that the key to a successful practice is never to lose your determination. Such a resolute approach is very important. The story of the Buddha's personal life is the story of someone who attained full enlightenment through hard work and unwavering dedication.

*I*f people everywhere are not allowed
to strive for the happiness they
instinctively want, then they will be
dissatisfied and will make problems for
everyone. Unless we can create an
atmosphere of genuine cooperation —
cooperation not gained by threat or
force but by heartfelt understanding —
life will become ever more difficult. If
we can satisfy people at a heart-level,
peace will ensue. Without the basis of
coexistence, if undesirable social,
political and cultural forms continue
to be imposed upon people,
peace becomes difficult.

Stealing harms others' property and welfare, and disturbs their peace and happiness. When a house is built, an ugly screen and iron bars are put on the windows to protect what is inside from thieves. Have you ever thought how just the sight of those bars, that screen, makes us uneasy and steals some of our peace and happiness?

*B*y maintaining sharp awareness of the function of religion as expressed in the actuality of all teachings, we can escape the ruinous error of sectarian discrimination and partisanship, and we can avoid the grave sin of casting aside any religious teaching.

*I*f there is love, there is hope to have real families, real brotherhood, real equanimity, real peace. If the love within your mind is lost, if you continue to see other beings as enemies, then no matter how much knowledge or education you have, no matter how much material progress is made, only suffering and confusion will ensue. Human beings will continue to deceive and overpower one another. Basically, everyone exists in the very nature of suffering, so to abuse or mistreat each other is futile. The foundation of all spiritual practice is love. That you practice this well is my only request.

When a day seems to be long, idle gossip makes our day seem shorter. But it is one of the worst ways in which we waste our time. If a tailor just holds the needle in his hand and goes on talking to a customer, the tailoring does not get finished. Besides, the needle might prick his finger. In short, meaningless gossip prevents us from doing any kind of work.

We eschew the path of mundane power, for the healing power of the spirit naturally follows the path of the spirit; it abides not in the stone of fine buildings, nor in the gold of images, nor in the silk from which robes are fashioned, nor even in the paper of holy writ, but in the ineffable substance of the mind and the heart of man. We are free to follow its dictates as laid down by the great teachers — to sublimate our heart's instincts and purify our thoughts. Through actual practice in his daily life, man well fulfils the aim of all religion, whatever his denomination.

November

*R*egardless of race, creed, ideology, political bloc (East and West), or economic region (North and South), the most important and basic aspect of all people is their shared humanity — the fact that each person, old, young, rich, poor, educated, uneducated, male or female, is a human. This shared humanness and thus the shared aspiration of gaining happiness and avoiding suffering as well as the basic right to bring these about, are of prime importance.

*O*ppression has never, anywhere, succeeded in suppressing the eternal desire of people to live as free men — free to think their own thoughts, free to act as they consider best for the common welfare and live as human beings — not as robots or slaves. Even if the Chinese leave nothing but ashes in our sacred land, Tibet will rise from these ashes as a free country even if it takes a long time to do so. No imperialist power has succeeded in keeping other people in colonial subjection for long.

*I*t is most unlikely that
we shall actually be able to
take on the sufferings of others
and give them our happiness.
When such transference
between beings does occur
it is the result of
some very strong unbroken
karmic connection
from the past.

*T*he practice of morality,
which means guarding your
three doors of body, speech and mind
from indulging in unwholesome
activities, equips you with mindfulness
and conscientiousness. Therefore,
morality is the foundation of the
Buddhist path.

*O*ur intention should not be spoiled by the eight worldly preoccupations: gain or loss, pleasure or pain, praise or criticism, and fame or infamy.

*N*othing is more important than guarding the mind. Let us constantly keep watch over the wild elephant of the mind, curbing it with mindfulness and vigilance. This is how one can avoid being influenced by different external conditions. But even in retreat in a very secluded place, if the mind is not kept under control, it will wander all over the place. Even when completely alone, we can have an enormous amount of negative emotions.

We have been and are still
going through endless suffering
without deriving any benefit whatever
from it. Now that we have promised
to be good-hearted, we should try not to
get angry when others insult us. Being
patient might not be easy. It requires
considerable concentration. But the
result we achieve by enduring these
difficulties will be sublime. That is
something to be happy about!

Aggression is an intimate part of ourselves. That is why we have to struggle. Men raised in a strictly non-violent environment have managed to become the most horrible butchers. This proves that the most insane aggressiveness continues to live in the depths of us. But our true nature is calm. We all know that the human mind is agitated, subject to frightful jolts. But this agitation isn't the dominant force. It is possible and necessary to master it.

*C*an the mind even see the mind? We have to answer yes and no. No, because the mind can't be a subject and object at the same time. The mind interferes, whether it wants to or not, whether it knows it or not, in all that it observes; and with all the more reason when it is a question of itself. But the mind cannot see itself completely. However, the principal tool for purifying the mind is the mind itself. The mind is its own creator, at every instant. Hence its responsibility, which is essential.

*L*onging for eternity exists because we cherish ourselves and provided our daily life is happy. But if it is miserable then you want to shorten life.

I believe that to meet the challenge of the next century all human beings will have to develop a greater sense of universal responsibility. Each of us must learn to work not just for his or her own self, family or nation, but for the benefit of all mankind. It is very old-fashioned to think in terms of my nation, or my country. Universal responsibility is the real key to human survival. Large human movements spring from individual initiatives. Thus it is the individual working for the common welfare who makes the difference.

The countless stars and constellations that we see today were gradually formed and discovered, but the interesting thing is that the more powerful telescopes we use, the more we will find — more and more stars and lives. Thus, the more we have power to see things, the more there is to see.

A person who knows a lot but does not practice is like a shepherd who does not own any cattle but always looks after a flock of sheep or cattle. Therefore, studying, reflecting and meditating on the nature of reality is of great significance for the progress of a spiritual practitioner.

Speech and bodily activities which accompany mental process must not be allowed to run on in an indiscreet, unbridled, random way. Just as a trainer disciplines and calms a wild and wilful steed by subjecting it to skilful and prolonged training, so must the wild, wandering, random activities of body and speech be tamed to make them docile, righteous and skilful. Therefore the teachings of Lord Buddha comprise three graded categories for disciplining the mind: Shila (Training in Higher Conduct); Samadhi (Training in Higher Meditation); and Prajna (Training in Higher Wisdom).

To be angry at hearing other people speaking highly of one's enemies is totally inappropriate, because at least in the mind of the person who is praising this enemy, there is some sense of fulfilment, some satisfaction. That person is doing so because he or she feels joyous and happy, and one should rejoice in that because one's enemy has caused someone to be satisfied. If possible one should also join in the praise rather than trying to obstruct it.

*T*here are two types of prayer. Prayers are, for the most part, simply reminders in your daily practice. So, the verses look like prayers but are actually reminders of how to speak, how to deal with problems, other people, etc. In my own daily practice, prayer takes about four hours. My practice is reviewing: compassion, forgiveness and shunyata.

Then, the major portion is the visualization of deity, mandala and attendant tantric practice including visualization of death and rebirth. In my case, it is done eight times. So, eight times death is eight times rebirth. I am supposed to be preparing for my death. When actual death comes, whether I will succeed or not, I don't know.

*I*n modern scientific terms, physicists, in their pursuit of understanding the nature of physical reality, have reached a stage where they have lost the concept of solid matter; they can't come up with the real identity of matter. So they are beginning to see things in more holistic terms, in terms of inter-relationships rather than discreet, independent, concrete objects.

Occasionally people who do not have a proper knowledge of karmic law say that such and such person is very kind and religious, but he always has problems, whereas so and so is very deceptive and negative, but always seems very successful. Such people may think that there is no karmic law at all. There are others who go to the other extreme and become superstitious, thinking that when someone experiences illness, it is all due to harmful spirits. However, there is a definite relation between causes and effects: that actions not committed will never produce an effect; and that once committed, actions will never lose their potentiality.

*G*enerosity is of three types: giving material aid, giving Dharma, and protecting from fear. 'Giving Dharma' refers to the giving of teachings to other sentient beings with pure motivation to benefit them.

When we pray together, I feel
something, I do not know whether you
would call it blessings, or grace — but
in any case there is a certain feeling
that we can experience. If we utilize it
properly, this feeling is very helpful for
developing our inner strength.

*I*n dealing with those who are
undergoing great suffering, if you feel
'burn-out' setting in, if you feel
demoralized and exhausted, it is best,
for the sake of everyone, to withdraw
and restore yourself. The point is to
have a long-term perspective.

*L*ook at one person who annoys you, and use the opportunity to counter your own anger and cultivate compassion. But if the annoyance is too powerful — if you find the person so repulsive that you cannot bear to be in his or her presence — it may be better to look for the exit! Here is the principle: It is better not to avoid events or persons who annoy you, who give rise to anger, if your anger is not too strong. But if the encounter is not possible, work on your anger and develop compassion by yourself.

*T*he mind can and must transform itself. It can get rid of the impurities that contaminate it, and rise to the highest level. We all start off with the same capacities, but some people develop them, and others don't. We get very easily used to the mind's laziness, all the more easily because laziness hides beneath the appearance of activity: we run right and left, we make calculations and phone calls. But these activities engage only the most elementary and coarse levels of the mind. They hide the essential from us.

We are all here on this planet, as it were, as tourists. None of us can live here forever. The longest we might live is a hundred years. So, while we are here we should try to have a good heart and to make something positive and useful of our lives. Whether we live just a few years or a whole century, it would be truly regrettable and sad if we were to spend that time aggravating the problems that afflict other people, animals and the environment. The most important thing is to be a good human being.

*B*uddha is the teacher, Dharma is the actual refuge and the Sangha is the one which assists in understanding or establishing the objects of refuge.

*O*rdinary compassion and love give rise to a very close feeling, but it is essentially attachment. As long as the other person appears to you as beautiful or good, love remains, but as soon as he or she appears to you as less beautiful or good, your love completely changes. Even though your dear friend is the same person, he feels more like an enemy. Instead of love, you now feel hostility. With genuine love and compassion, another person's appearance or behaviour has no effect on your attitude. Real compassion comes from seeing the other's suffering. You feel a sense of responsibility, and you want to do something for him or her.

*I*f we examine ourselves every day
with mindfulness and mental alertness,
checking our thoughts, motivations and
their manifestations in external
behaviour, a possibility for change and
self-improvement can open within us.
Although I myself cannot claim with
confidence to have made any
remarkable progress over the years, my
desire and determination to change and
improve is always firm. From early
morning until I go to bed and in all
situations of life, I always try to check
my motivation and be mindful and
present in the moment. Personally, I
find this to be very helpful in
my own life.

*D*o your best and do it according to your own inner standard (call it conscience), not just according to society's knowledge and judgement of your deeds. 'To do our best' is just a phrase of a few words, but it means that at all times in our everyday life we should check our mind so that we don't feel guilty about our mistakes, even though others don't know about it. If we do that, we are doing our best.

*I*t is important to think very well before entering a particular spiritual tradition. Once you have entered you should stick to it. Do not be like a man who tastes food in all the different restaurants but never actually gets down to eating a meal. Think carefully before adopting a practice; then follow it through. This way you will get some results from dedicating even a little time each day. Alternatively, if you try to follow all the various paths you will not get anywhere.

*I*t seems that when men become
desperate they consult the gods. And
when the gods become desperate, they
tell lies!

December

*I*rrespective of whether we are believers or agnostics, whether we believe in God or Karma, moral ethics is a code which everyone is able to pursue. We need human qualities such as moral scruples, compassion and humility. Because of our innate human frailty and weakness, these qualities are only accessible through forceful individual development in a conducive social milieu, so that a more humane world will come into being.

*N*ow I am always quite cheerful! It is, I think, the result of my own practice and training. In my lifetime, I have lost my country and have been reduced to being totally dependent on the goodwill of others. I have also lost my mother, and most of my tutors and gurus have passed away, although I now have a few new gurus. Of course these are tragic incidents, and I feel sad when I think about them. However, I don't feel overwhelmed by sadness. Old, familiar faces disappear, and new faces appear, but I still maintain my happiness and peace of mind.

*I*f a person has a really deep interest in
spiritual growth, he or she cannot do
away with the practice of meditation.
That is the key! Just a mere prayer or
wish will not affect this inner spiritual
change. The only way for development
is through a constant effort through
meditation. Of course, in the beginning
it is not easy. You may find difficulties,
or a loss of enthusiasm. Or perhaps in
the beginning there will be too much
enthusiasm — then after a few weeks
or months, your enthusiasm may wane.
We need to develop a constant,
persistent approach based on a
long-term commitment.

When we talk about violence, we must understand that we are speaking about a phenomenon in which it is almost impossible to predict the outcome. Even though the motivation on the part of the perpetrator of the act may be pure and positive, when violence is used as a means, it is very difficult to predict the consequences. For this reason, it is always better to avoid a situation that may require violent means. However, tolerance and patience do not imply submission or giving in to injustice.

*T*he person who has a tremendous reserve of patience and tolerance has a certain degree of tranquillity and calmness in his or her life. Such a person is not only happy and more emotionally grounded, but also seems to be physically healthier and to experience less illness. The person possesses a strong will, has a good appetite, and can sleep with a clear conscience.

*I*f you help others with sincere
motivation and sincere concern, that
will bring you more fortune, more
friends, more smiles, and more success.
If you forget about others' rights and
neglect others' welfare, ultimately you
will be very lonely.

*F*rom the perspective of the highest dimension of Buddhist practice, the Highest Yoga Tantra, there is no distinction between gender. Even in that final life in which you attain Buddhahood, there is no difference whether you are male or female. There are more female concerns in this system. For example, one of the root downfalls is for a male to abuse or to look down upon a female. If a man does that, it is disastrous. There is no comparable downfall for a woman looking down on a man.

So we men are jealous.

*I*t is not enough to be compassionate. You must act. There are two aspects to action. One is to overcome the distortions and afflictions of your own mind, that is, in terms of calming and eventually dispelling anger. This is action out of compassion. The other is more social, more public. When something needs to be done in the world to rectify the wrongs, if one is really concerned with benefitting others, one needs to be engaged, involved.

I normally recommend to Buddhist practitioners not to see every action of their spiritual teacher as divine and noble. There are specific, very demanding qualities that are required of a spiritual mentor. You don't simply say, 'It is good behaviour because it is the guru's.' This is never done. You should recognize the unwholesome as being unwholesome, so one might infer that it is worthwhile to criticize it.

*I*f one feels very profound compassion, this already implies an intimate connection with another person. It is said in our scriptures that we are to cultivate love just like that of a mother towards her only child. This is very intimate. The Buddhist notion of attachment is not what people in the West assume. We say that the love of a mother for her only child is free of attachment.

*P*eople should remain in society and carry out their usual profession. While contributing to society, they should internally carry on analysis and practice. In daily life, one should go to the office, work and return home. It would be worthwhile to sacrifice some late evening entertainment, go to sleep early, and get up early the next morning to perform analytical meditation.

*T*o help others in the most effective
way possible we have to be
fully enlightened buddhas. Even to
help others in vast and extensive ways
we need to have attained one of the
levels of a bodhisattva, that is, to
have had the experience of a direct,
non-conceptual reality of voidness
and to have achieved the powers of
extra-sensory perception. Nonetheless,
there are many levels of help
we can offer others.

*F*rom one point of view
we can say that we have
human bodies and are practising
the Buddha's teachings and are thus
much better than insects. But from
another view we can say that insects
are very innocent and free from guile,
whereas we often lie and misrepresent
ourselves in devious ways in order to
achieve our ends or better ourselves.
From this perspective, we are
much worse than insects, who just
go about their business
without pretending
to be anything.

*I*n this age of degeneration when one meets with all sorts of problems and adverse circumstances, the practice of generating positive thoughts is very effective. If someone lacks this practice, even though that person might be a very serious meditator he or she will meet with many hardships and hurdles.

*L*et us examine what 'I' or 'self' is. What is definite is that it does not exist independently of our body and mind. And out of the two, the body and mind, it is clear that the body cannot be seen as this 'self'. Feelings are also not the self because there is a 'feeler' and a feeling. Also, the way we naturally perceive ourselves, the way the sense of 'self' arises, is that there is something like the agent or the subject, which experiences and perceives. So to our naive, natural mind, everything appears as if it has an independent, solid, objective entity or objective status. However, what is very clear is that when we begin to search, they disintegrate and disappear, and they are unfindable.

We are all on this planet together. We are all brothers and sisters with the same physical and mental faculties, the same problems and the same needs. We must all contribute to the fulfilment of the human potential and the improvement of the quality of life as much as we are able... Mankind is crying out for help. Ours is a desperate time. Those who have something to offer should come forward. Now is the time.

*I*f you know that someone is speaking badly of you behind your back, and if you react to that negativity with a feeling of hurt, then you destroy your own peace of mind. One's pain is one's own creation. One should treat such things as if they are wind behind one's ear. In other words, just brush them aside. To a large extent whether or not one suffers pain depends on how one responds to a given situation. What makes a difference is whether or not one is too sensitive and takes things too seriously.

*I*n most cases the affirmation of the ego leads only to disappointment, or else to conflict with other egos just as exclusive as mine — especially when the strong development of the ego leads to whims and demands. The illusion of the permanent self secretes a danger that lies in wait for all of us: I want this, I want that. You might end up killing someone, as we all know well.

The excess of egoism leads to uncontrollable perversions, which always end badly. But from another standpoint, a firm ego, sure of itself, can be a very positive element. You have to have real confidence in yourself.

You have to understand that the affection I am speaking of has no purpose, it is not given with the intention of getting anything back. It is not a matter of feeling. In the same way we say that real compassion is without attachment. Pay attention to this point, which goes against our habitual ways of thinking. It is not this or that particular case that stirs our pity. We don't give our compassion to such and such a person by choice. We give it spontaneously, entirely, without hoping for anything in exchange. And we give it universally.

*I*f I die in exile,
and if the Tibetan people wish
to continue the institution of
the Dalai Lama,
my reincarnation will not
be born under Chinese control.

With the love that is
simply attachment, the slightest
change in the object, such as a tiny
change of attitude, immediately causes
you to change. This is because
your emotion is based on something
very superficial. Take, for example,
a new marriage. Often after a few
weeks, months or years the couple
become enemies and finish up
getting divorced. They married deeply
in love — nobody marries with
hatred — but after a short time
everything changed.
Why?

*S*ome psychologists say
that we should not repress
anger but express it — that we
should practise anger! Here we
should make a distinction between
mental problems that should and
should not be expressed. Sometimes
you may be truly wronged and it is
right for you to express your
grievance instead of letting
it fester inside you. But you
should not express
it with anger.

*I*f you go more deeply into your own spiritual practice, emphasizing wisdom and compassion, you will encounter the suffering of other sentient beings again and again, and you will have the capacity to acknowledge it, respond to it, and feel deep compassion rather than apathy or impotence. When contemplating suffering, do not fall into the feeling of self-importance or conceit. Cultivating wisdom helps us to avoid these pitfalls. But it is hard to generalize because each person's courage and forbearance are unique.

*T*he self-cherishing attitude
makes us very uptight; we think
we are extremely important, and our
basic desire is for ourselves to be happy
and for things to go well for us. Yet we
don't know how to bring this about. In
fact, acting out of self-cherishing can
never make us happy.

No matter who we are with,
we often think things like
'I am stronger than him', 'I am more
beautiful than her', 'I am more
intelligent', 'I am wealthier', 'I am
much better qualified', and so forth —
we generate much pride. This is not
good. Instead, we should always remain
humble. Even when we are helping
others and are engaged in charity work,
we should not regard ourselves in a
very haughty way as great protectors
benefitting the weak.

*I*f you must be selfish, then be
wise and not narrow-minded
in your selfishness.

Whoever excludes others will find himself excluded in turn. Those who affirm that their God is the only God are doing something dangerous and pernicious, because they are on the way to imposing their beliefs on others, by any means possible.

*T*here were once two monks — a teacher and his student. In order to give some encouragement to his student, the teacher said, 'One day we will definitely go for a picnic.' After a few days it was forgotten. The student later reminded the teacher of his promise but the teacher responded by saying that he was too busy to go for a picnic for a while. A long time passed; no picnic. When reminded again, the teacher said, 'Not now. I am far too busy.' So one day the student saw a dead body being carried off, and the teacher asked him, 'What is happening?' And the student replied, 'Well, that poor man is going on a picnic!' So, unless you make specific time for something that you feel committed to, you will always have other obligations.

*T*he essence of all spiritual life is your emotion, your attitude toward others. Once you have pure and sincere motivation, all the rest follows. You can develop this right attitude toward others on the basis of kindness, love and respect and on the clear realization of the oneness of all human beings.

I would like, on behalf of the Tibetans, in and outside Tibet, to sincerely thank our supporters and friends. When we are going through immeasurable hardship and suffering which is unprecedented in our history, the sympathy, support and help that the people of the world, led by India, have accorded to us will forever be remembered and recorded in history.

*F*or as long as space endures,
and for as long as living beings remain,
until then may I, too, abide,
to dispel the misery of the world.

INDEX

Action

Whether in remote . . . 21

When a faulty . . . 22

On the basis . . . 23

Ideally, one should . . . 48

Every noble work . . . 56

It looks like . . . 89

When we are . . . 169

Buddha has never . . . 188

In the present . . . 221

One of the . . . 229

The advantage of . . . 253

Just as rust . . . 282

Negative actions have . . . 316

Occasionally people who . . . 352

It is not . . . 374

Activities

Speech and bodily . . . 348

Advertising

If advertising is . . . 126

Affection

The main cause . . . 171

One aspect of . . . 190

You have to . . . 385

Aggression

Aggression is an . . . 342

Altruism

Compassion, tolerance and . . . 81

If in a . . . 113

Happiness is man's . . . 137

The modern economy . . . 145

First we must . . . 202

Great compassion and . . . 219

Anger

It would be . . . 19

For discovering one's . . . 41

A nagging sense . . . 65

Subconscious anger, if . . . 80

At the moment . . . 84

People who fight . . . 128

I myself still . . . 146

INDEX

Many people think
. . . 157
Anger and hatred . . .
172
When we encounter . . .
186
There are many . . . 256
When people get . . . 276
When one is . . . 313
Look at one . . . 356
Some psychologists
say . . . 388

Art
The training of . . . 211

Attachment
For discovering
one's . . . 41
It objects and . . . 53
The idea that . . . 64
When we encounter . . .
186
There are different . . .
217
In Buddha's time . . .
314
If one feels . . . 376

Attitude
Everything has its . . .
57
What irritates us . . . 58
If we are . . . 120
When a problem . . . 216
When receiving
the . . . 240

It seems to . . . 247
There is no . . . 317
The essence of . . . 395

Authority
The ultimate authority
. . . 140
We do not . . . 295

Awareness
To foster inner . . . 7
It seems to . . . 106
Tranquil or calm . . .
198

Beauty
Good motivation
causes . . . 150

Blessings
In Tibetan, the . . . 241
Blessings are not . . .
264
When we pray . . .
354

Bodhicitta
Bodhicitta is the . . . 110
Such practies as . . . 112
There is a . . . 292

Bodhisattva
For a bodhisattva . . . 91
To help others . . . 378

Body
It is said . . . 31

INDEX

Try to develop . . . 73
When one
meditates . . . 315
Speech and bodily . . .
348

Bombs
In the case . . . 222

Buddha
When we take . . . 98
The Fully Enlightened
. . . 109
Natural environment
sustains . . . 118
Buddha has never . . .
188
Great compassion
and . . . 219
We do not . . . 295
Buddha advises: 'O . . .
305
In Buddha's time . . .
314
As a spiritual . . . 325
Buddha is the . . . 359

Buddhahood
Whatever we say . . .
119
Buddhahood is a . . .
178
There is a . . . 292

Buddhist notions
There is said . . . 230

Vegetarianism is
very . . . 239
The criterion that
. . . 243
An area in . . . 302
The void, shunyata,
. . . 309
The practice of . . . 338

Buddhist practice
Whenever Buddhism
has . . . 116
From the
perspective . . . 373

Calm
Tranquil or calm . . .
198

Censorship
It is difficult . . . 249

Cessation
I used to . . . 158
We can speak . . . 238

Change
If you want . . . 63
If we examine . . . 361

Charity
One important type . . .
99

Circumstances
There are many . . . 209

INDEX

Cloning
    Cloning is an . . . 183

Community
    As far as . . . 191

Compassion
    In the case . . . 12
    True compassion
    is . . . 40
    Whether one
    believes . . . 69
    Compassion, tolerance
    and . . . 81
    I have found . . . 105
    Compassion can be . . .
    153
    One aspect of . . . 190
    Great compassion
    and . . . 219
    We must each . . . 237
    The creatures that . . .
    262
    Since we have . . . 279
    Human beings are . . .
    287
    Only a spontaneous . . .
    319
    Look at one . . . 356
    Ordinary compassion
    and . . . 360
    If one feels . . . 376
    You have to . . . 385
    If you go . . . 389

Consciousness
    During conception,

    even . . . 44
    Your experience will
    . . . 61
    Today our knowledge
    . . . 82
    The grosser
    consciousness . . . 108
    Samsara—our
    conditioned . . . 129
    According to its . . . 236
    In the case . . . 254

Continuity
    Samsara—our
    conditioned . . . 129

Contradictions
    Within oneself,
    within . . . 192

Cooperation
    For a bodhisattva . . . 91
    The modern economy
    . . . 145
    If people everywhere
    . . . 326

Crime
    It may surprise . . . 122

Death
    If you are . . . 6
    When we contemplate
    . . . 72
    Such practices as
    . . . 112
    If a patient . . . 130

INDEX

The dying process . . .
131
In the case . . . 254
We are afraid . . . 281
There is no . . . 291

Death penalty
I am absolutely . . . 248

Delusion
In one sense . . . 162
We learn from . . . 176
Delusion is a . . . 220

Demilitarization
Another issue which
. . . 310

Desire
Sexual desire by . . . 87
There is a . . . 149
In one sense . . . 162
I am sometimes . . . 163
Regarding
inter-gender . . . 258
Oppression has
never . . . 325

Dharma
The Fully
Enlightened . . . 109
As a result . . . 252
Buddha is the . . . 359

Differences
The differences in . . .
125

Within oneself,
within . . . 192
All the waters . . . 303

Discipline
Cultivating
inner discipline . . . 127
Discipline is a . . . 165

Earth
The earth is . . . 197
Just like the . . . 275

Education
Kindness is the . . . 26
Our whole
educational . . . 246

Ego
In most cases . . . 384

Effort
There are three . . . 260

Emotions
There are many . . . 256
Our judgements,
even . . . 286

Endeavour
What is endeavour . . .
182

Enemies
It would be . . . 19
Unlike an external . . .
208

INDEX

To be angry . . . 349

Enlightenment
   As long as . . . 45
   What is reborn . . . 323

Ethics
   In the correlation . . . 204
   Irrespective of whether . . . 367

Exile
   Kindness is the . . . 271
   Exile has helped . . . 308
   Now I am . . . 368
   If I die . . . 386

Existence
   A blossoming tree . . . 27
   When I doubt . . . 147
   Dreams are an . . . 177
   While one possesses . . . 259
   Just as rust . . . 282

Faith
   Faith dispels doubt . . . 187
   We speak of . . . 324

Faiths
   I believe in . . . 205

Fame
   We should not . . . 155

Family
   Kindness is the . . . 26
   We are born . . . 141
   Wise parents, without . . . 306
   Whether their entire . . . 288
   A limit to . . . 271

Fear
   If you have . . . 4
   When you have . . . 59
   I find that . . . 159

Feeling
   When we pray . . . 354

Friendship
   We have genuine . . . 154

Gender
   Regarding inter-gender . . . 258
   From the perspective . . . 373

Generation
   I tell my . . . 24
   Among the 5.7 . . . 46

Generosity
   We can hardly . . . 29
   Generosity is of . . . 353

Giving
   I understand

INDEX

the . . . 107
While you are . . . 152
Generosity is of . . . 353

God
It seems to . . . 247
It seems that . . . 364
Whoever excludes
others . . . 393

Gossip
When a day . . . 330

Greed
If an individual . . . 90

Guilt
Guilt, as experienced
. . . 179
Guilt, according to . . .
251

Guru
It is often . . . 144
If students sincerely
. . . 214
The guru, the . . . 223
As students, you
. . . 283
I normally recommend
. . . 375

Happiness
All living beings . . . 17
Human happiness and
. . . 38
The world today . . . 74

Happiness is a . . . 86
One important type
. . . 99
Happiness is man's
. . . 137
A very poor . . . 175
One of the . . . 229
Human beings are
. . . 287

Harmony
One of the . . . 121
Anger and hatred
. . . 172

Hatred
A nagging sense . . . 65
Anger and hatred . . .
172
There are many . . . 256
When one is . . . 313

Heart
A good heart . . . 123
Human beings are . . .
287

Help
As long as . . . 45
It is necessary . . . 103
The task of . . . 269
If you help . . . 372
To help others . . . 378

Human nature
If the basic . . . 43
One of the . . . 121

❋   405   ❋

INDEX

One aspect of . . . 190
The three physical . . .
273
If any sensible . . . 322
From one point . . . 379

Human potential
Human potential is . . .
75
We are all . . . 382

Human relations
Human relations
based . . . 206
The task of . . . 269
It is vital . . . 285

Human rights
Peace is of . . . 201

Humanity
Physically you are . . .
11
It seems to . . . 106
The modern
economy . . . 145
In the case . . . 185
To remain
discouraged . . . 189
Human beings are . . .
287
Regardless of race . . .
335
We are all . . . 358
Irrespective of
whether . . . 367

Humility
No matter who . . . 391

Ideals
Ideals are very . . . 138

Ignorance
The metaphor of . . . 294
There is no . . . 317

Impatience
Cultivating inner
discipline . . . 127

Impermanence
Some people, sweet . . .
49

Impression
Sometimes one
creates . . . 16

Indifference
Since we have . . . 279

Individuals
Individuals who are . . .
62
If an individual . . . 90
If we consider . . . 148
The ignorance,
arrogance . . . 307

Insight
Tranquil or calm . . .
198

INDEX

The metaphor of . . . 294

Interdependence
When we consider
. . . 70
In our world . . . 95

Intimacy
I don't have . . . 196

Introspection
For discovering
one's . . . 41
The image we . . . 88
Taking your own . . .
111
A strong sense . . . 115

Joy
One of the . . . 229

Judgements
Our judgements,
even . . . 286

Justice
I believe in . . . 205
If any sensible . . . 322

Karma
If the evolution . . . 85
If in a . . . 113
Due to karmic . . . 203
One of the . . . 229
The truth of . . . 242
In Buddha's time . . .
314

It is most . . . 337
Occasionally people
who . . . 352

Killing animals
Years back when . . . 92
Vegetarianism is
very . . . 239

Kindness
Right from the . . . 8
Kindness is the . . . 26
Whether one
believes . . . 69
For a bodhisattva . . . 91
The creatures that . . .
262

Knowledge
As long as . . . 45
Today our
knowledge . . . 82
Crucial to the . . . 161
The metaphor of . . . 294

Lawbreakers
Stealing harms others'
. . . 325

Laziness
Laziness will stop
. . . 47
There are three . . . 260

Lessons
It may surprise . . . 122

INDEX

Life
Simply being
praised . . . 30
When we
contemplate . . . 72
Natural environment
sustains . . . 118
It is possible . . . 257
One great question . . .
270
Perhaps in
monasteries . . . 274
Longing for eternity . . .
344
We are all . . . 382
The essence of . . . 395

Light
According to tantra . . .
79
The metaphor of . . . 294

Listening
It is through . . . 151
I am talking . . . 296

Logic
Anything that
contradicts . . . 293

Love
Nearly all of . . . 52
The idea that . . . 64
On the subject . . . 71
If a person . . . 160
If there is . . . 329
Ordinary compassion
and . . . 360
With the love . . . 387

Mahayana
Crucial to the . . . 161

Man
It seems to . . . 106
Man and society . . . 301
We are all . . . 382

Marriage
On the subject . . . 71
With the love . . . 387

Media
The power of . . . 210

Meditation
Scientific research
and . . . 9
The human level . . . 15
To develop genuine . . .
25
We practise various . . .
50
When we contemplate
. . . 72
To stop being . . . 97
One of the . . . 121
It is necessary . . . 170
In the meditation . . .
173
For a meditator . . . 215
To overcome
attachment . . . 272
Our experience

INDEX

is . . . 298
If a person . . . 369

Mental conflict
I feel there . . . 320

Mind
To develop genuine . . .
25
It is said . . . 31
Our state of . . . 51
Both bondage and . . .
55
According to tantra . . .
79
If an individual . . . 90
The mind whose . . . 93
Suffering originates
from . . . 94
It is because . . . 96
One important type . . .
99
I understand the . . .
107
The grosser
consciousness . . . 108
You should see . . . 156
It is necessary . . . 170
In the meditation . . .
173
The training of . . . 211
Delusion is a . . . 220
It is possible . . . 257
To overcome
attachment . . . 272
Western brains
work . . . 289

In the case . . . 311
Nothing is more . . . 340
Can the mind . . . 343
Speech and bodily . . .
348
The mind can . . . 357

Misdeeds
When a faulty . . . 22

Misery
A skilled physician . . .
265
For as long . . . 397

Mother
Nearly all of . . . 52
The earth is . . . 197
The fact remains . . .
228
If one feels . . . 376

Motivation
On the basis . . . 23
Politicians need
religion . . . 33
Good motivation
causes . . . 150
I find that . . . 159
When we talk . . . 193

Nirvana
Samsara—our
conditioned . . . 129

Non-violence
On the basis . . . 23

INDEX

Swords can be . . . 143

Omniscience
When receiving the . . .
240

Path, the
Encountering
sufferings will . . . 164
We can speak . . . 238
While one possesses . . .
259
The metaphor of . . . 294
As a spiritual . . . 325

Patience
To develop patience . . .
20
We need to . . . 76
Many people think . . .
157
There are different . . .
318
When we talk . . . 370
The person who . . . 371

Peace
Peace is of . . . 201
Human beings are . . .
287

Perfection
When we talk . . . 193

Perspective
In dealing with . . . 355

Politicians
Politicians need
religion . . . 33

Possibility (prajna)
One thing can't . . . 184

Power
The countless stars . . .
346

Practice, spiritual
According to
Buddhist . . . 39
Individuals who are . . .
62
To stop being . . . 97
One important type . . .
99
It is necessary . . . 170
Regarding my
actual . . . 231
When we practice . . .
235
One should enter . . .
255
In addition to . . . 261
In the beginning . . . 312
As a spiritual . . . 325
We eschew the . . . 331
A person who . . . 347
There are two . . . 350
It is important . . . 363
Now I am . . . 368
From the
perspective . . . 373

INDEX

Persons should remain
... 377

Practitioner
True practitioners
are ... 244
As a result ... 252
A person who ... 347

Prayer
Regarding my
actual ... 231
There are two ... 350

Problems
All the problems ... 124
When we are ... 169
Today we face ... 227
The growth in ... 278
Make efforts to ... 304

Progress
Material progress
alone ... 14
If we consider ... 148

Qualities
Determination, courage
and ... 28
Three qualities
enable ... 114
If you rely ... 212
It is possible ... 257
If you are ... 290
Irrespective of
whether ... 367

Reality
In modern scientific ...
351

Reasoning
To foster inner ... 7
The ultimate
authority ... 140

Rebirth
In the cycle ... 250
There are two ... 350

Reconciliation
One aspect of ... 190
Within oneself,
within ... 192

Relationships
I sometimes think ...
213
Regarding inter-
gender ... 258

Religion
All of the ... 10
In the case ... 12
I think religion ... 13
Religion involves
practice ... 32
According to the ... 78
The very purpose ...
135
By maintaining
sharp ... 328

INDEX

Responsibility
  The observation
  that . . . 104
  We know that . . . 136
  In the present . . . 221
  I believe that . . . 345

Rituals
  When through
  rituals . . . 224

Samsara
  According to tantra . . .
  79
  Samsara—our
  conditioned . . . 129
  In the cycle . . . 250

Sangha
  Buddha is the . . . 359

Satisfaction
  Human happiness
  and . . . 38
  If one's life . . . 77

Science
  Scientific research
  and . . . 9
  It seems to . . . 106
  In modern scientific . . .
  351

Self
  The image we . . . 88
  Emptiness should
  be . . . 117

  Let us examine . . . 381

Self-awareness
  To be aware . . . 5
  We must each . . . 237

Self-examination
  In this
  ever-changing . . . 60
  Do your best . . . 362

Self-improvement
  If we examine . . . 361

Selfishness
  According to the . . . 78
  Should we persist . . .
  218
  The self-cherishing
  attitude . . . 390
  If you must . . . 392

Sexual desire (see Desire)

Sexual misconduct
  Sexual misconduct
  has . . . 225

Slander
  To be aware . . . 5

Sleep
  If during the . . . 18
  We practise various . . .
  50
  In addition to . . . 261

INDEX

Smiles
  I love friends . . . 3

Society
  Material progress
  alone . . . 14
  To renounce the . . . 37
  Man and society . . . 301
  People should
  remain . . . 377

Speech
  To be aware . . . 5
  Speech and bodily . . .
  348
  If you know . . . 383

Spiritual master (see
  Teachers, spiritual)

Spiritual practice (see
  Practice, spiritual)

Spiritual teaching (see
  Teachings)

Study
  To study a . . . 180
  As a result . . . 252

Success
  Determination, courage
  and . . . 28
  Rather than being . . .
  207
  When one

  meditates . . . 315

Suffering
  Suffering increases
  your . . . 42
  Suffering originates
  from . . . 94
  Encountering
  sufferings will . . . 164
  We learn from . . . 176
  Some people might . . .
  181
  The truth of . . . 242
  When things are . . . 245
  I feel there . . . 320
  It is most . . . 337
  We have been . . . 341
  In dealing with . . . 355

Tantra
  According to tantra . . .
  79
  In one sense . . . 162
  A single word . . . 195
  From the
  perspective . . . 373

Teachers, spiritual
  When we take . . . 98
  The Fully
  Enlightened . . . 109
  A spoilt child . . . 139
  The advantage of . . .
  253
  As students, you . . . 283
  I normally

INDEX

recommend . . . 375

Teaching(s)
Three qualities
enable . . . 114
Crucial to the . . . 161
For a meditator . . . 215
When others insult . . .
226
When receiving the . . .
240
A skilled physician . . .
265
I find that . . . 297
Speech and bodily . . .
348

Technology
Western brains
work . . . 289

Tendencies
Leaving aside
memory . . . 277

Thought
In this age . . . 380

Tibet
I believe in . . . 205
A real 'Tibethood' . . .
280
An area in . . . 302
Oppression has
never . . . 336
I would like . . . 396

Tibetan medicine
Here is a . . . 54
In the Tibetan . . . 142
On one occasion . . . 174

Time
We find that . . . 83
Time never waits . . .
194
There were once . . . 394

Tolerance
When we talk . . . 370
The person who . . . 371

Training
Speech and bodily . . .
348

Truth
The world today . . . 74
I am talking . . . 296

Understanding
As a result . . . 252
Great vigilance
must . . . 321
In modern scientific . . .
351

Unity
The differences in . . .
125

Violence
On the basis . . . 23

INDEX

It may surprise . . . 122
Since we have . . . 279
When we talk . . . 370

Waste
Try to develop . . . 73

Western society
Overall I have . . . 263
Perhaps in monasteries
. . . 274

Wisdom
Crucial to the . . . 161
Great compassion
and . . . 219
There are three . . . 284
The metaphor of . . . 294
If you go . . . 389

Wishes
What irritates us . . . 58

Words
I myself still . . . 146
When others insult . . .
226
I am talking . . . 296

World
To renounce the . . . 37
Nowadays the
world . . . 132

Worldly preoccupations
Our intention
should . . . 339

Women
There is a . . . 292
From the
perspective . . . 373

Youth
Among the 5.7 . . . 46